Self-Esteem for Women

The Ultimate Self-Help Guide to Building Habits that Will Improve Your Confidence, Self-Compassion, Assertiveness, Self-Love, and Mindset

Contents

Introduction

Has your self-esteem taken a hit over the last couple of years? Perhaps you even remember back in childhood being made to feel small, and that feeling of smallness stuck. The fact is that the self-esteem of a woman is vital to her happiness. It is the backbone that she depends upon to come across to others as a complete and confident person. Is it possible to improve your sense of self-esteem? Indeed, it is, but you need to know how to do it, and that's where this book comes in handy. Years of work with women who deal with self-esteem and confidence problems have gone into writing this book, and you want to turn the page knowing that if you do, you can change your life.

Many women make the mistake of ignoring this aspect of their lives, yet it can make the difference between happiness and unhappiness in a huge way. It can also make a difference in the way that others approach you as a woman. Have you ever wondered why some women get teamed up with losers? What about those that get into abusive marriages? It isn't a coincidence that most of these women have emotional problems brought about by self-esteem issues. Is it their fault? Not at all. It's simply that they have not yet discovered ways in which to help their self-esteem levels to rise. In fact, if you want a backup of the importance of self-esteem, you need to look no further than the psychological theory diagram that was made in the '40s by Abraham Maslow. What he said is still relevant; he gave a list of things that people need within their lives to be happy and to make the most of their lives. One of the items on this list is self-esteem and the appreciation of others, while the uppermost item on the list is self-actualization. What does this mean? It means what's on the label! It means making the most of who you are as a woman who is very happy with her life, knowing it's going in the direction she intended.

This book was written and designed specifically for women. The advice and tips that are contained within it will help you to move out of that zone of discomfort into a better place so that you can face the world with your head held high, knowing that you maximize your life and are happy with the results of your efforts. Self-confidence and self-esteem are never far behind when you can do this. Even though you may have self-doubts at this moment, while you are reading the introduction, the chapters within this book will certainly take you where you want to go. Your life lies out ahead of you. There's a child inside you. There's also a goddess, waiting for you to recognize her needs. Once you do, you will surprise yourself because your potential stretches much further into the horizon than you may imagine. Take this journey and know that you are not on your own. There are others with you every step of the way, and reinforcement comes in that nod of approval you give yourself in the morning as you start your day. It also comes from what you get back from life when you put your best foot forward. People around you will notice the butterfly that is emerging and will want to share that victory with you.

Lastly, in this introduction, I will tell you a secret. Your life is only beginning. If you thought that you would have to hide behind damaged self-esteem forever, then the book will prove to you how wrong that perception is. You have so much power to change your life and to become the woman you always wanted to be. Let the book be your guide to self-realization as the woman you were always intended to become awaits. There is no time like now to take that leap of faith.

That's where this book comes into play. The books deal with the problem of self-esteem from a woman's perspective and help readers to perform exercises and activities that will help them to build themselves back up again. Stop being a victim to life and start taking your life to another level. This book will help you to do just that. You may be surprised at the determination and courage that is hiding within you.

Chapter One: Self-Esteem Psychology 101

"We use language to create realities. Use it to create a version of you that you love." –Mariella Dabbah

What makes a woman suffer from self-esteem issues? Well, contrary to what you may find on some websites, women don't automatically suffer from this in adolescence. They may go through it as they grow, but it's not simply something that happens because a girl is growing up. Some girls grow up with a super sense of identity and never experience self-esteem issues at all. They fly through their lives and find happiness is very easy to achieve, while others struggle. Others may have an over-the-top level of self-esteem that you could call uber-ego, and that's not healthy. Let's have a look at some major signs of self-esteem issues that you can go through as a checklist to see whether what you believe you are suffering from is actually self-esteem related:

☐ You feel pessimistic and don't expect good things to happen to you

☐ You crave approval from other people

☐ You feel you are unworthy of other people's love

☐ You don't like yourself very much

☐ You tend to self-sabotage and never really follow through

☐ You may blame others for your misfortunes

☐ You may seek sympathy and occasionally act the drama queen

☐ You may not look after yourself as well as you should

☐ You may seek your security in other people

☐ You may be lazy when it comes to making friendships

☐ You may be a bit of a pushover when it comes to being used by others

If you can relate to any of these, then perhaps you need to look further, and this book will explain what's happening when any of these are applicable in your case. Each girl is born with the same amount of self-esteem. However, what happens in your life and how you relate to others around you will dictate how you respond to life and how much self-esteem you retain. Self-esteem can be mended if, for example, you find that you suffer from any of the above symptoms. It's simply a case of following the habits shown in a later chapter. For now, write down which of these you believe applies to you because you are currently making yourself aware of a problem, and that's a good thing. Once you admit the problem, solving it becomes easier and less painful.

Think of this 101 as your introduction to self-esteem issues and understand that just because you suffer from one or more of the above symptoms doesn't mean you are past redemption or that you can't do anything to change any one of them. You can, but it will take a little work on your part to put these things right so that you face the world on equal terms. It's a great feeling when you know that you don't have to measure up to other people's standards and that you can simply be you. This has always been the case, but as stated earlier, your experiences through the course of your life dictate how you respond to life and can be the underlying causes of self-esteem issues. You may not have been loved in the way that you hoped, or perhaps you didn't love yourself. Regardless of this, the symptoms apply to you in one way or another, or you would not have been browsing books on Amazon trying to find solutions.

☐ You feel pessimistic and don't expect good things to happen to you

In the case of feeling like this, perhaps you are accustomed to things going wrong. Here you can use the example of someone who has been made to believe that they are clumsy. They will believe that they are clumsy, and as a result, will find that their approach to life actually makes them clumsier than someone who does not believe themselves to be clumsy. Self-esteem works on experiences, and if you feel pessimistic, perhaps it's because you are approaching life with a bleak view because of experiences that you have been through in your life. Perhaps you suffered from parental disapproval, or you failed your exams. Perhaps you have failed relationships in your past and expect nothing short of a disappointment, which is what feeds your pessimism. The other reason why people use pessimism is as a shield. If you don't expect anything, then you can't be disappointed. However, as far as self-esteem goes, this approach is self-defeating. You do need to believe in yourself, and so pessimism isn't an option.

You may suffer from a pessimistic attitude because of other things. Perhaps you were brought up to expect nothing, but now you are an adult, and there are many things that you should expect as standard to your life. These words are important, so make a note of them. You should expect RESPECT FROM OTHERS, RESPECT FROM YOURSELF, and THE CHOICE IN LIFE TO AGREE OR DISAGREE when people want you to accept things that you question in your mind. The fact is that although someone else may be more knowledgeable than you, no one has the right to dictate the life that you live, and you will find out that the only person holding you back in this respect is you. Perhaps you lack the assertiveness actually to speak your mind, but that's okay too. We will show you how to deal with this throughout the chapters in the book. You must read it all, rather than jumping forward to find solutions, because the better your understanding of self-esteem, the more likely you are to understand the solutions being offered in a later chapter.

☐ You crave approval from other people:

This is more common than you may think. When you don't have confidence in yourself, you tend to look elsewhere for it. People with self-esteem issues do this because it makes them feel validated. However, they have not yet learned to validate themselves so that they don't need external validation. This is a bad habit that doesn't feed self-esteem at all. You may think that asking your boss if you did a good job will give you positive feedback, but you will already know you did a good job, so why do you need his validation? People who crave this kind of attention have problems finding the validation they need within themselves. There are some exercises later in the book that will help you to deal with this and to learn to approve of yourself above all else because that approval is your steppingstone to confidence. The validation that you get from others is momentary, and the feeling of achievement does not last. Only when you validate yourself does it become part of who you are and go with you through your life. You are an individual and should need no validation from anyone else at all. You should know your saving graces as well as your potential errors, but many people go through their lives seeking validation because they don't believe that self-validation works. It does, and it works better and longer-term to help you to overcome self-esteem issues.

☐ You feel you are unworthy of other people's love:

This can quite regularly stem from feeling unloved by people you trusted to love you. It may be that you believe yourself unworthy of love because people you love seem to be treating you in that way. Thus, it must be so. However, although relationships that are not positive can lead to self-esteem issues of this kind, they don't have to. You have to learn self-love, and that's a tough lesson for someone to learn when they are beginning to deal with self-esteem. Don't be concerned. This book will show you how self-love happens and how you can work toward it. This area of the book also deals with people who don't like themselves very much because they lack self-love. You may be the woman that sits in the corner at parties, not expecting anything to happen. You may be the person who doesn't even go to parties because you feel out of your depth in a social environment. However, you haven't yet learned to unleash the goddess inside you, and we will also discuss this later in the book. No one is unworthy of love. If you believe that, then it makes the world a potentially bleak place. Remember, even the people who make bad choices were loved at some stage in their lives. Whatever you have done in life and whatever you have had done to your emotions, this is fixable, but you need to learn to let go and move forward.

☐ You tend to self-sabotage and never really follow through:

A lot of people who don't follow through do this because they are afraid of disappointing themselves and others. The lack of confidence comes from a lack of self-esteem and can be looked at from another angle. What would be the worst-case scenario if you failed? Do you have to be good at everything? The fact of the matter is that there are things you can be good at and with which you can follow through. You just haven't found them yet. The other way to look at this is that you may just be afraid of success. That may sound a little weird, but when a singer brings out a wonderful record and never produces anything like it again, it can spell the end of their career. Similarly, people are afraid to take that first step because it's hard enough, and they don't know if they can keep to that high standard that people will expect of them. In the case of a promotion, some women sit back and avoid it because they don't want to be made to look foolish by not being able to live up to others' expectations. Look at situations in your life and ask yourself what stopped you from succeeding, and it's almost certain that your approach had something to do with that failure-based attitude.

☐ You may blame others for your misfortunes:

In this case, you blame others because it's easier than facing up to the fact that you didn't do the things in your life that you wish you had done. The fact is that a lack of self-esteem can hold you back, and sometimes it's easier to point the finger at someone else than it is to stop and examine your actions. I once knew a relative who did this all of her life. She was exceptionally talented, but instead of going on the stage and becoming a well-known concert pianist, she used other people as her excuse for not doing it. "My mother never really encouraged me", was one of the excuses. "I had to go out and get a paying job", was another excuse. All the time, she felt resentment because she had failed to live her dream, but never really saw herself as her own stumbling block. It was easier to blame the birth of her children or the attitude of her husband than it was to look to her own personal failure to let her inner self shine. Her self-esteem was low, and it was this that made her so thoroughly unpleasant to people around her, while she could have taken to the stage and would have indeed enjoyed a very worthwhile career had she made that choice. At the end of the day, blaming others for your misfortunes doesn't help you to get beyond them. It is your reaction to circumstances that will generally affect you if you have self-esteem issues.

☐ You may seek sympathy and occasionally act the drama queen:

There's a big problem with this one. I have dealt professionally with people who have suffered from this, and at the time of playing the drama queen, they were not really aware that they were doing this. The reason why women do this is to draw attention away from the real problem. Don't worry if you have been guilty of this. Many women do this in an attempt to gain attention, and although they don't know their motives, they are usually pretty innocent ones. They do not use drama for the sake of manipulation. They simply use it because their lack of self-esteem wants to make them look more important in the eyes of the world that is seemingly ignoring them. The young girl who runs away may not hate home but may just be trying to be noticed amid a growing family. A girl who wears black lipstick and goes Goth isn't doing it to annoy people. She is doing it because she is trying to find her own style and personality, but not looking inward at who she really is. Self-esteem won't be earned in this way. It simply twists the thoughts in your mind even more than they are now, and honestly facing up to who you are is the first step toward self-realization and love.

☐ You may not look after yourself as well as you should:

Do you know why women do this? Within their heart and soul, they believe that they should give their attention to others more than thinking about themselves. To a certain extent, it's endearing because other people feel that these are very caring people. But if you stop caring for yourself, eventually it catches up with you, either in the form of stress or anxiety, and you will reach a point where you need to look after yourself more than you do others. You were not born to be a martyr, to give up on important things for the sake of others. There's being kind, and there's being neglectful, and when you are kind and look after yourself correctly, then you will find that the mix is a far healthier one for not only you but the people around you. Imagine going into a relationship while being someone YOU consider as incomplete or not worthy of looking after. Does that mean that your partner is obliged to do all those things for you? The point here is that to help build up your self-esteem, you don't need the approval of others, but you do need your self-approval, and this will be more likely to follow if you respect yourself and look after yourself as you should. Anything less than that, and you are offering a relationship a partly built person instead of a fully developed and capable person.

☐ You may seek your security in other people:

This point, as well as the last two, is all about becoming someone else's doormat. You please people because you don't know how to please yourself and have not yet gained the confidence to say "no." You feel incomplete without a partner in life and try not to spend too much time alone. You feel that you are part of a relationship but that without the other part, you cannot continue. However, this is something that you do need to address, and we will show you how. The problem with this manner of thinking is that it leaves you open to being abused by people around you who will take advantage of the fact that you need them more than they appear to need you. When you can even out the odds, you will find more people need you for all the right reasons, and you can leave those who use you behind. You will also find that your own company is not as frightening as you first thought. When you find self-love, your own company is often enough, and even when you are in a loving relationship, you don't feel frightened of being alone. You appreciate that you and your partner are both WHOLE people without needing someone else to support them, though you do appreciate the love that you get from a partner who is also WHOLE.

The book will lead you through these dilemmas and show you how to deal with them as well as help you to find your best self so that you never need to worry about self-esteem again. Do I expect you to have any doubts? Of course. Everyone is entitled to doubt something from time to time, but if the core of your being is solid, then the doubts are overcome easier and don't become the focus of your life. That's the difference between a woman with self-esteem and one who has none. Don't worry, if you have read this far, you have miles to go, but the book will tell you how to do all these things, and you won't be completely on your own while you work toward the transition from a woman with self-esteem issues to one who is confident in herself and her abilities, her beliefs, and her likes and dislikes. You have a whole treat ahead of you, so turn the page and bear with me.

Self-Esteem Includes the Following Elements

☐ The ability to depend upon yourself

☐ The ability to be dependable

☐ The ability to try new things

☐ The ability to say "no" when this is your choice

☐ The ability to avoid clinging to people

☐ The ability to recognize your achievements

These are the facets that we will be working on together through the course of this book, and the whole purpose is to help you to see yourself as the whole person that you are, rather than letting self-esteem get in the way of building fruitful and enjoyable relationships with others. People with self-esteem issues can't do this because they have too many doubts. There are ways to stem those doubts, and this will also be covered within the coming chapters. If you have read this far and are beginning to recognize yourself as being someone with self-esteem issues, don't be afraid to turn the pages, as they hold a huge amount of potential for you to become that person you always wanted to be. We all have this ability, and there are no exceptions. There are no excuses and no reasons why you cannot be the star of your own life. When you become that star, you will be recognized by others for the beautiful person that you are, and that's when life starts to happen.

Chapter Two: Self-Esteem versus Self-Confidence

"When you start seeing your worth, you'll find it harder to stay around people who don't" ~ Unknown.

Self-esteem is what you think of yourself. Inflated self-esteem means that you are perhaps acting in a superior way, and this can be a problem. Low self-esteem means that you don't put enough attention into the caring equation when it comes to looking at the most important person in your life – and that's you.

Although you may be tempted to see both of these problems as being the same, they are not. Yes, there are similarities, but you can lack confidence without having a lack of self-esteem. Situational anxiety can make you feel a lack of confidence, although as soon as you are over that situation, you may not experience that lack of confidence again until another anxious moment happens. However, someone with self-esteem problems will demonstrate this in various ways.

Self-Confidence

If you have self-confidence, you are unlikely to feel uncomfortable in a social situation. You are happy in the skin you are in and carry yourself in such a way that people can clearly see that you have a grown-up head on your shoulders, and a lack of confidence does not impair your approach to life. Self-confidence is affected by what you know, and some people may feel a lack of confidence while they are learning new things. While these situations may produce self-doubts, the difference between this and a lack of self-esteem is that the doubts only usually last until that hurdle is overcome. These are signs of self-confidence:

☐ You are happy to do things on your own

☐ You are happy with your learning abilities

☐ You are happy around people and can easily fit in with new people

☐ You are happy with your place in the world

☐ You don't find it too hard to learn new things

☐ If you fail in something you do, you don't mind

☐ You like yourself in general

☐ You have friendships that are give-and-take, and understand friendship.

Self-confident people appear to be happy in their lives and are willing to try new things. They are likely to have more ambition than those with self-esteem issues and will relate to others better than those who are always looking inward at themselves as not fitting in. If you lack confidence, it's usually focused in an outward direction rather than being negatively biased against you; you will adjust to situations, and once you have adjusted, you will no longer lack confidence. It's a normal state of affairs. Imagine that you are about to meet your boyfriend's parents for the first time. You love your boyfriend, and you naturally want to make a good impression. The girl who lacks confidence will want to find it by logical means, by talking and trying to impress in a simple way. She won't doubt her abilities. She doesn't show herself to be uncomfortable but accepts that the situation may make her feel a little out of her depth. She will most likely seek the advice of her boyfriend about what she should wear, not wishing to underdress or overdress. She will simply doubt the situation until it becomes more comfortable. The person with self-esteem issues has more to worry about because the problem isn't just what those parents think of her, but that she will overreact in an attempt to correct the things that she feels are wrong with her, and that can come over in a different way that is less acceptable.

Self-Esteem

We were all born with equal self-esteem. However, it is affected by the way that people around us perceive us. We take feedback from our interactions with others, and sometimes that feedback is negative. Whereas a person who has self-confidence problems needs to overcome the hurdle of learning something new, someone who has self-esteem issues will look for validation from other people because they find no validation from within themselves. People with high self-esteem may show these traits:

- ☐ They have carefully set boundaries

- ☐ They know their capabilities

- ☐ They can trust themselves

- ☐ They can do things on their own

- ☐ They are confident and sure of themselves

Why would someone with high self-esteem need boundaries? Because they know what acceptable behavior is to them, and they will accept nothing less than that. All human beings need boundaries, although those with lower self-esteem sometimes feel that they don't have the right to create boundaries and thus show themselves to others as being easy prey. Let me explain a few obvious boundaries, and you can expand on them, so you can see why they are created, and in fact, how they are created. When you become a teen girl who is developing breasts, you may wish to have more privacy in the bathroom or the shower. That's perfectly normal and part of growing up. In the case of a child who has learned to use the potty, that child may feel that he doesn't want to wear diapers anymore because it makes him feel like a small person when he has earned the right not to wear them. This last point is a little exaggerated, as most parents will know, but the idea of showing it was to demonstrate that at all ages we create boundaries. We don't want our brothers and sisters playing with our things without permission. We learn to say, "thank you" and "please", but as an adult, you have to look at the overall picture of your life and create solid boundaries that other people respect. Typically, acceptable boundaries existing throughout your life are those such as:

- ☐ Don't look in my handbag. It's private.

- ☐ Don't use my phone without asking me first.

- ☐ Don't choose my clothes for me.

- ☐ Don't treat me like a servant.

These are all reasonable boundaries, and once the people around you accept that these represent acceptable behavior to you, then they respect them. If they don't respect them, you can complain to them that your boundaries are not being respected and expect them to apologize. We create boundaries because we all have a private bubble around us. Have you ever been on a train and had someone's coat pushing against you and taking up your space? Well, it's natural that you don't want strangers impeding upon your personal space, but it also works in the same way with boundaries. There are acceptable and unacceptable behaviors; finding out what these are and making them known helps people around you to respect you and to respect the boundaries set.

Someone with high self-esteem usually likes their own company and doesn't mind being left out of social situations. They are happy to do things on their own and feel that those who wish to be anti-social have the problem rather than it being their own problem. However, when that self-esteem is lacking, then people can use an individual to such an extent that he/she may feel like they are being treated like a doormat (but are unlikely to do anything to change that, as it's what they expect). Thus, defining boundaries becomes quite important for people who suffer from self-esteem issues, and the solutions will be discussed in future chapters. Boundaries stop things like this from happening and define your rules in life. If you don't want to babysit every Saturday night for the rest of your life, make it clear that you need some Saturdays for you. You make the rules in your life, and you do not permit others to use you in a way that is detrimental to your own personal growth.

There is a clear distinction between self-esteem and self-confidence. Although someone who lacks confidence may be shy in new situations, it's likely to be because of the unknown, whereas the person who has self-esteem issues will not want to socialize because they feel they are undeserving or don't fit in. These are two different attitudes, but both produce that feeling of inadequacy in one way or another. To get over one, you have to deal with the other. Thus, working on self-confidence can help a person to gain self-esteem, and vice versa.

Observe people for the next week and see who you would classify as being confident and who you would say has self-esteem issues. You need to focus outside of yourself sometimes to see how the world works. This isn't your solution; it's merely a tip to help you to see people for who they are so that you get a better idea of the difference between self-esteem issues and lack of confidence.

A person with confidence will not need time to answer a question. A confident woman isn't afraid of being heard. However, someone with self-esteem issues may not have the same reaction because a lot of their thought processes are inward so that they don't always make themselves aware of what is happening around them. Ask someone who has confidence in what they are good at, and they will not hesitate to tell you their passions and strong points. However, a person with self-esteem issues may struggle to find anything they can boast about, even if they are good at certain things.

Look at the way that people present themselves. This is interesting. You may have two women who dress identically, but the confident one will always shine when the two are compared. Body language comes into the picture at this stage, and you can instantly recognize confident posture as compared to the posture of someone with self-esteem issues. Look at the high heels. Does she walk proudly in them, or does she stumble because she is unsure of herself? Look at the body language. Does one woman stand straighter than another? The fact is that you don't actually have to speak to be recognized as being someone with a lack of self-esteem. The actions of your body will give it away.

Who are you? Who do you want to be? Who are you capable of being? All of these are relevant questions because they help to make you into who you show to observers in your life, and that makes a whole heap of difference to the way that you live your life and interact with others.

Look at people's smiles as well. This gives you a clue as to how confident they are. Does the smile come from true feelings of self-worth? If it does, you will know it. However, if it's a nervous smile, it can give the impression that self-esteem may be an issue. There are many kinds of smiles, so, over the next week, see if you can distinguish the differences – look for sincerity, nervousness, and insincerity. A smile can convey all of this, and you will begin to see how posture and the movement of facial features make a huge difference in how you are perceived.

"Smile, for everyone, lacks self-confidence and more than any other one thing a smile reassures them." ~ Andre Maurois

Chapter Three: Meeting Yourself – Identifying who YOU Really Are

"A good guy will tell you that you are beautiful. A real gentleman will make you believe it!" ~ Anon

Have you ever asked yourself who you are? For the sake of this exercise, I want you to sit and think about it for a moment and find all of the adjectives that you can to describe who you think you are. You know you can use whatever words you like, as no one is going to read this. It's an exercise simply to demonstrate something of which you may be unaware.

Now, look at the words that you have used to describe yourself and place them into two separate columns. One side will show all the positive things that you have to say about yourself, and the other side will list all the negative things that you said about yourself. I would bet that the negative side is longer than the positive side. That's because a large portion of all of the thoughts that we think each day is negatively biased. In the old days, when our caveman ancestors had to protect themselves from huge creatures, it was self-preserving to think negative thoughts. It kept them on their toes and made them very aware of the danger. However, those dangers don't exist today, but we still think in the same negative way, and people think this is our self-defense mechanism against getting hurt. However, it doesn't quite work in that way.

You have approximately 70,000 thoughts per day, and these conversations that go on in your head start from the moment you wake up. If you get up on the wrong side of the bed, you can have negative thoughts flood your mind all day long. It's not uncommon. Now, let's look at the list you made of all the negative things you thought about yourself. Surely, there will be a fair number of negative attributes that you put down to being you.

I want you to pick up this list, and look at the length of it, and then fold it in half and tear it into shreds. Place the paper in the bin. That's what your thoughts are worth at this moment in time. You thought them, and then they were gone. You defined yourself in words and believed that those words accurately described who you are. But have you ever thought that they are just thoughts and that they don't have any bearing on the reality of who you are? Who you are is much more complex than that, and your thoughts don't make or break you unless you let them.

Besides, the things that you think can change. Suppose I was to ask you the same thing just after you met a man whom you believe is going to become the love of your life? Your answers would be different. Suppose I asked you just after you received a letter that said that you didn't get the job you were after. The answers would once again change, but you are still the same person. In fact, every moment of your life is different, and the way you feel about yourself differs as well, which means that the value of these negative thoughts is zero. You don't improve yourself by merely looking at your thoughts unless you learn something from them.

If you have self-esteem issues, you may already think that you know who you are; even if you only have confidence problems, you probably have a vague idea of where this chapter is going. However, I want you to think in a new way, and that's the part that is not going to seem natural to you for the time being. Bear with me as you start on this new journey because I want to show you the power of thought, and your power over what those thoughts do to your mind.

How the Brain Works

To understand better, you have to understand a little more about the structure of the brain and which parts of the brain tell you to be wary when you are placed in a situation that makes you uncomfortable. It's the hippocampus area of the brain, and it records all of the things that appear important to you. It monitors your activities and looks for repetitions in your behavior because it sees those as being pretty important to you. As you grow up, you learn to say "please" and "thank you" at the appropriate times, and by now probably do that without even thinking about it because they are habits that have been recorded in the hippocampus. The hippocampus takes a lot of mental work out of your life and will do things automatically before you even have time to think about them. Thus, if you think bad things whenever you are in a situation where you need confidence, then that part of the brain will automatically switch to making you think things like:

- I am not good enough
- I can't do this
- I am clumsy
- I am not worthy

The thoughts are all coming from you. But what if the thoughts were different? Well, they can be. When you face situations with a different attitude and start to respond to social situations with positive statements, your hippocampus records those positive responses and will use these as your normal responses in the future. Just as you learned to say "please" and "thank you", you will learn to respond positively to the things that happen in your life. The thoughts are not worth anything until you start using them to reinforce who you are rather than trying to make yourself less of a person.

Begin to wonder what would happen if you treated your thought patterns differently. For example, when negative thoughts happen, imagine yourself switching the volume down so that you can no longer hear the negative words being said. Then on occasions when you see something positive about yourself, imagine turning the volume up and basking in those positive thoughts. What you are feeding to your hippocampus is the fact that you believe in yourself and are building your self-esteem and confidence.

If I was to ask you to write down the things that you like about yourself, you might not be able to think of that much. That's because you are not accustomed to doing this, and if you hang out with people who are also negative toward you, chances are they reinforce all those negative feelings that you have... but what if this could change? It can, and the way that the lady in the video above did it was to gather her clients around her and learn to accept compliments from the other people who formed that circle. You and I don't have that circle, but we do have the ability to do the same thing. If you spend time with people who are positive toward you instead of those who are negative, you gradually start to build a much different picture, simply by learning to chalk up those compliments and thank people for them. Mentally note when you get compliments, and for this exercise, I want you to go through the next week and instead of thinking about the negative things about yourself, celebrate the positive things that people say about you and the things that you find yourself thinking that are positive affirmations of who you are and what you like about yourself.

Spend Time with Supportive People that Love You for Who You Are

This is important because it's your reinforcement. When people believe in you, you begin to realize that you can't be all bad. Otherwise, they wouldn't be in your life. Perhaps they have their motives for being there, but these are people who are willing to give and take in a relationship and who are there for you when you need someone to be. It doesn't matter how many friendships you have or whether you are the most popular girl on the block. None of that matters because one friendship that is solid and reinforcing is better than ten friendships that you cannot depend upon. Ask your friends about who they see you as, just like the lady did in the video, and explain why you are doing it beforehand. Someone else in your group of friends may even want to join in to help her to increase her confidence or self-esteem level. Make sure that they don't think that you are fishing for insincere compliments, but write up a list of questions and listen to their responses so that you get to see who you are from the point of view of people you like. Some of the questions could be the following:

- Do you see me as a nice person?
- Do you think that I am pretty?
- Do you think that I am a positive addition to your life?
- What can you tell me about the positive side of my character?
- What would you say are my strengths?

Delete the negative thoughts and boost the volume on the positive ones, and don't forget to say "thank you" for the feedback that your friends give you, whether it appears to be positive or negative. The thing is that these people are trying to help you with your insecurities, and all of their feedback has value. If you get any negative feedback, you can turn down the volume or, since these are good friends, you can examine the answers and see how you can use those answers to turn negativity into positivity. People with self-esteem issues take things far too personally, and that's because they are half expecting negative feedback but don't know what to do with it when it happens. However, if you learn what to do with constructive negative feedback, you help yourself to develop as a human being. If the negative feedback is something you can do nothing about, turn down the volume. For example, you can do nothing about your height. You can do nothing about your accent or physical traits that are built-in. Perhaps you could improve on those, but you can't change genetic physical things about yourself, so you shouldn't take negative feedback to heart. Ask yourself if it is something you need to learn from, and if there is nothing to learn, switch off the volume.

There's a practice called mindfulness, which is very useful for people who feel that they lack confidence or self-esteem. Although it wasn't invented for this purpose, it does help people to become happier and healthier. When you think something positive about yourself, boost it. Write it down in your journal. Carry a journal with you everywhere and use this to read through before you go to bed at night. This will reinforce the positive thoughts that you had about yourself that day. Perhaps you thought, "I like the shape of my nose", or "I like that I am not the same as everyone else", or anything at all that is positive. Now to deal with the negative self-image, you need to train your hippocampus to see reactions which it isn't expecting, and that's where mindfulness comes in.

When you feel negative thoughts, instead of letting them take over your feelings, switch them off. Use mindfulness to do this. It's very simple. Breathe in and count to 7 and while you are doing this, let go of the thought. Breathe out and notice things around you at this moment in time. Look at colors, smell aromas, touch something, and be in the moment, replacing negative thoughts with positive input from your feelings. It isn't the easiest thing in the world to do at first, but as I said, the hippocampus is recording your reactions, and after a while of doing something or responding differently it will automatically kick in and create a new habit; after that, it's plain sailing because once a habit is established, it takes work to get rid of it. So banishing negative self-talk and replacing it with being in the moment is a far more constructive way to deal with the negativity you feel about yourself before you go into an exam room or when you don't think you will get the job you are applying for. While breathing, hold your head up high, so breathing is made easier, and let the breath cancel out the negative thought. You can use this in moments of stress as well because this type of breathing helps you to contain panic and let go of it. Thus, you are in control of it, and once you realize this, you will find that negative thoughts don't have a lot of impact on your panic buttons anymore.

The Two-Way Mirror

Have you ever thought about what people see when they look at you? The fact is that they see an unbiased view of a human being, but what if you could give them more than that? Imagine that every person in the world goes through all the negative thought processes that you do, and learn to compliment and be kind to others. Have you ever seen what happens when you smile at someone? Usually, unless they are stressed out and in a world of their own, they smile back. A radiant smile is returned to us a thousand times a day, and it's a wonderful thought that those around us see us in such a positive light. Be kind to friends. Be supportive of friends and don't be afraid of compliments because, in this way, you are not just building up who you are, you are also improving the lives of others.

The two-way mirror effect is rather clever. If you are genuinely complimentary to someone you know, you feel good about what you said, and they feel good about it too. They also feel positively toward you, and this shows in the way that they react. That reaction comes back to you, and so it goes on until you start to see a better image of yourself emerging. Welcome to who you are. Embrace who you are and take pleasure in being that human being that makes a difference in the lives of others, and in doing so makes her own life better.

When you say thank-you for a compliment you are given, you are acknowledging it and using it to create positive thoughts in your mind. So do others. Simply be grateful for compliments you receive and thank that person for the thought. Then pay it forward to someone else. We can't change the world that we live in without making changes in the way we perceive ourselves. When you have the confidence to tell someone that her hair looks nice or that her dress is lovely, you are doing more than that; you are spreading confidence, and that never hurt anyone. The other thing that you are doing is viewing something in a very positive way, which makes you feel good about being you. You can't fail to feel good about yourself when you are friendly to people and ask nothing in return for your compliments.

Think of the two-way mirror. You see a human being in the mirror, but the mirror is looking back at you. Others notice the way that you present yourself, so imagine the mirror from both sides so that you build up the image that others get. It's a little like a magnet for positivity, but one that doesn't include allowing yourself to be used by people when nothing is coming back. You don't need physical validation, because the validation you get comes from a happy hippo who sees you as someone who positively responds to life. The next time that you find yourself feeding the hippocampus with misery or self-doubt, just think of feeding the poor creature with positivity, so that you begin to live with a happy hippo instead of one who perpetually reminds you that you lack in some way.

Meeting yourself head-on can be a little scary, but you can get over those initial fears, start to examine the good parts of your personality, and work from there. Look after how well your hair looks, and even go as far as taking care of those toenails. Every part of this person is you, and you are now meeting yourself head-on and understanding a little more about yourself through self-examination. If you know that you neglect something, it's okay. Everyone does, but that doesn't mean you can't work to improve your image or to change your situation as time passes. The person that you meet today will be someone else tomorrow, but the underlying core will be the same. You need a stable base upon which to stand, and after that, life will become easier for you.

Look in the mirror and see yourself for the first time in all your glory. You are a wonderful human being and go far beyond what is seen on the surface. Now, you are going to start to get to know the different elements that make you who you are. This is the only way that you can change your approach and learn self-love, and indeed, self-appreciation. It doesn't mean becoming vain. It means appreciating who you are and learning that you can make the most of who you are simply by changing a couple of stray habits.

An interesting thing to note in this regard is that the social butterfly from schooldays probably isn't the most successful person in the world these days. As you grow, perspectives change, and different things come into play. I once knew someone who was terribly unpopular at school, and the other girls were relentless in their teasing of her. However, instead of turning inward and shrinking, it taught her to be compassionate and kind, and she now has a career doing exactly what she loves – looking after people who need help. Your future isn't bleak. Your lack of self-esteem doesn't spoil it. When you meet the person that you'll become when you lose your self-esteem problems, you will be very proud of that person. You will become proud of who you are and what you stand for because it's a natural follow-on from learning about your interactions with others and changing small things about yourself that matter to you.

When you meet yourself in the mirror, always be honest. Always appreciate the good things about yourself and try to do something about things you are not happy about. Remember, it's more than the surface. It's all about who you are inside, so stop trying to change things over which you have no control. The surface looks, your height, your complexion is all part of being you and are as individual as all women should be. You have attributes that others don't have. You have depth, and you have courage. How do I know that? I know that because you are still reading and still learning about how to see yourself from a neutral perspective so that you can make yourself into anyone that you want to be. This is who you are.

Chapter Four: Self-Doubt – Spot it, Silence It!

"The moment you doubt whether you can fly, you cease forever to be able to do it." – J. M. Barrie

Have there been times in your life when you were obsessed with the idea that you couldn't do something? Most of us have felt like this at some time, but when you do this more often than you have positive thoughts, this can affect self-esteem and self-confidence. If you are accustomed to saying, "I can't," you are feeding the hippo with bad food. Think of the hippocampus as a huge hippo. When you feed him, you want to feed him positive things, because when he is grouchy, you get grouchy. He remembers and will always make you respond to circumstances in life in the way that he sees as your normal way. When you tell him regularly that this isn't the way you are going to respond, you change the habit of talking to yourself negatively. You have to spot self-doubt and eradicate it. That means showing the hippo that you don't have self-doubt and that it's so insignificant when it happens that you can laugh it off and move on.

I remember an aunt who could not knit. She tried very hard, but no matter how hard she tried, she simply could not do it. She was a wonderful woman, and this frustrated her to the extent that she got very negative about it. However, when she discovered a knitting machine, there was no stopping her. Mechanics was something that she understood. Life throws all kinds of opportunities into your path, but that's not to say that all of those opportunities are ones at which you will excel. Accept that you can't do everything and start to celebrate the things that you can do.

There are several methods that you can use to get rid of self-doubt, and some of these have been covered in previous chapters. However, it's worth keeping a shortlist, so that you can easily refer to it and practice what it says:

☐ Switch off negative thoughts.

☐ Share positivity.

☐ Keep a journal of things for which you are grateful.

☐ Keep on looking within yourself for things you admire.

☐ Recognize what others say to you in the way of compliments.

☐ Learn from mistakes.

Make your own notes of several other things you can add to this list.

When you build molehills into mountains, you are making your own life difficult, and usually, this is done based upon sheer speculation. Instead of doing that, look at events in the past and work out the answers to "What would be the worst that could happen?" Then, work out the *best* thing that could happen, and work toward achieving it so that mistakes from the past become lessons for today, and you don't continue to make the same mistakes. When you do make mistakes, look at these as life lessons.

How many times have you heard your friends say things like "I am not falling for that again" or "I am not interested in men anymore"? What they are doing is getting past bad situations and trying to move on, but they are also learning from bad experiences so that in the future, they don't fall into the same trap. It's okay to tell yourself that you are moving forward and don't intend to be caught out again, but it's not alright to stop your life based upon your bad experiences. If you do this, you tend to hide from the world instead of embracing it and the opportunities it offers. Self-doubt can be an awful thing, but most of the time, if you do logical calculations on the events that made you feel like that, you will find there is no fault on your part. It was just circumstances. So, move the hurdle out of the way and move on. Looking backward will always trip you up.

Self-Doubt is Self-Defeating

When you approach a situation with an attitude that things will go wrong, they probably will –but not for the reasons you think. You may think that things go wrong because of your part in those events when that's only a small part of the picture. The hippo is coming out to haunt you again, and this time, he's remembering things you did in the past and using these against you. To stop this from happening, feed the hippo with positivity even when you are worried about something. Start telling yourself that you can get through this, rather than defeating yourself by feeding yourself negative feedback about your past failures. I will show you how to do this in the chapter relating to habits because when you treat the hippo to great food or positive thoughts, you really can tame it to respond to life more positively.

The negative fodder that you feed the hippo is being remembered. Every time you come across a new situation the hippo will be responsible for your negative responses. Thus, start to show your brain that you are in charge and that you are not prepared to fail without putting up a fight. Think hippo, and care for your hippo sufficiently to tell it that there are positive answers to everything that you currently perceive as being negative.

Let me give you an example of the hippocampus at work, to prove to you how it works. If you stay in a house where you get out of bed on the right-hand side every day, and then stay elsewhere where you have to get out on the left, you will find that for the first few days your mind is disorientated because your automatic response cannot happen and it makes you feel out of sorts. As soon as you go back to your own bed and you get used to getting out on the right-hand side, you confirm that habit and the hippocampus tell you that's what you need to do in the morning. However, what if you moved to a new house completely and forever? Or even if you moved your bed to a different position. For the first couple of weeks, the hippocampus needs to be educated to that new position of the bed, and the repetition of getting out on the other side becomes a habit. Until that habit is established, you will feel odd about getting out on the wrong side of the bed, but once he has learned that's the way it's going to be from now on, you won't have problems. The hippocampus can be reprogramed, and this simple example was to explain how it works and how it acts upon the things that you do in the course of your day by habit.

I can give you a funnier instance. Having recently moved to a new house, when I go to the toilet in the middle of the night, my hand reaches up to the right to get the toilet roll. For nearly 30 years, that's where it was. It's an automatic reaction. The hippocampus has not yet accepted that the toilet roll has moved, and it is only by habit that it will relearn this. Thus, if you feed yourself negative feedback and self-doubt, the hippocampus sees that as your normal response to life, and it will take a little while to make it think otherwise... but it can be done.

Reframing

When you spot self-doubt raising its ugly head, think straight away about reframing the problem so that you see it in a positive light. For example:

"I can't"

is replaced by

"I can learn how to do that ".

"I am no good at this"

is replaced by

"I am great at ...".

The whole point is that no one is good at everything, and if you go through life believing that you have to be, you are in for a disappointment. Just accept who you are without letting self-doubt creep into your mind. You have your strengths. There are things about you that are unique. Don't let self-doubt become one of them!

For example, I can't run a tidy home. It is not who I am, but I don't kick myself for it because there are other things I can do and excel at. Stop trying to be everyone's ideal and begin to be happy that you are your own ideal. That makes life a lot easier, and as you do this and approve of your actions instead of doubting them, your brain is learning more about the self-confident side of your character. In the habit section of this book are exercises that will help you to reinforce your strengths and get over any kind of self-doubt that you have. Remember that thoughts are nothing but thoughts, but repeated thoughts form habits. The kind of habits that you need to develop are positive ones, rather than negative ones, so don't keep repeating negative statements to yourself because they are self-defeating and will only lead to more self-doubt.

If someone was to ask me if I could stand on a stage and play the violin, I would laugh rather than feel incompetent. I can play the violin, but it's been years since I even touched one, and even then, it was a hobby my parents wished on me, rather than one I wanted to pursue. I am not afraid of saying "no" to those things outside my area of comfort. If someone wanted me to stand on my head for half an hour, I could possibly do that and would be willing to try, but the mistake that human beings make is doubting their abilities when in fact, their abilities may just be different from those demanded by others. You have strengths, and I want you to write them down and remember them. You have things that you are good at. Write them down and celebrate them, but just because you can't do everything, don't beat yourself up about it. We all have things that we cannot do, and that doesn't make us wrong. It simply means that we have other priorities.

Self-doubt should never stop you from trying something. If you don't want to do it, say so, and move on. If you don't think it's something you are that good at, say so and move on, but stop trying to impress everyone into liking you. I like loads of people who can't cook. I like many people who are not as practical as I am. The point is that your self-doubt makes you into less of a person than you have the right to be. Start to praise the things you can do and laugh at the mistakes that you make or learn from them. Self-doubt eats away at your confidence and makes you feel that you don't measure up, but why do you have to? The whole point is that none of us measure up to other people's standards and nor do we have to. We just have to measure up to our own standards. You will learn how to do that by changing habits, and those habits will go a long way toward taking away any self-doubts that you may have.

Habits are the framework of your life, which is why a chapter has been put aside to introduce you to habits that will change your life. If you doubt that you can adapt, then have no fear. These are habits that are simple to perform, and you won't be expected to step outside of your comfort level. What you don't know is that you have many habits already and it's simply a case of changing your habits and adopting new ones that help you to move forward without looking back at the moments of your life which have been spoiled by self-doubt. By the end of reading this book, you will not only believe in yourself, but you will have all of the self-esteem you need to be able to excel.

Chapter Five: Fears, Anxieties and Insecurities

"Just when the caterpillar thought the world was ending, she became a butterfly." – Barbara Haines Howett

I want you to read the quotation above once more. The point is that there are times in your life when you read things wrong, and anxiety kicks in, when around the corner of chance lies the most wonderful discovery of all. You discover your capabilities, your dreams, your hopes, and your aspirations while anxiety is only a step away from that discovery. You just need help getting off this steppingstone and onto the next one.

Before we go further on this topic, you need to understand that all of the insecurities and anxieties that you feel come from inside your own head. That may sound a little harsh, but it's true. Yes, you may feel anxious about body image, but it's not the body image itself that is causing this. It's the way that you react to life in general after your emotions kick in to give their five cents' worth. Nothing that relates to anxiety and insecurity can do anything to your state of mind without the facilitation of emotions. Thus, if you control those emotions and know how they work, this helps you to build self-esteem and self-confidence. It's not how you look, but how your emotions carry you through certain situations that matter. Your mind may go into overdrive and feed you all kinds of negative statements that make sense to you at the time. Just like the caterpillar believed that it was the end of her life as she shed her coat, but discovered it was the beginning of something very beautiful, your anxieties are simply stepping stones to self-realization; learning to deal with them helps you to jump from one stepping stone to the next without becoming hurt in the process.

Your mind has set beliefs. Since you were a very small child, you have stored images in your mind concerning what you feel are acceptable pictures of who you should be. You have images such as:

☐ Someone who is confident

☐ Someone who is shy

☐ Someone who is motherly

☐ Someone who is cross or angry

☐ Someone who doesn't fit in

☐ Someone who is awkward and shy

Through the storybooks that you read as a child, you were introduced to all of these characteristics and know the difference between them, but it's very hard to visualize yourself when it comes to descriptions that are as intimate as this. The problem with these images is that somewhere along the line, you started to feel emotional because you didn't fit those images. That's what happens when self-esteem is low or when you don't have self-confidence. You may picture someone dressing in a certain way in your mind's eye or giving off certain body language based upon what your emotions know about it. The hippo has a huge memory. Perhaps you think of someone who is confident as a teacher that you had at school and measure yourself against that image. Perhaps you see the struggles of someone who is shy, and your personality avoids that trait. The point is that the whole of the human race has to come up against these differences every day; we see them in the people that we interact with and we start to set certain patterns that we feel are acceptable, and sometimes we find ourselves disappointed because we feel we don't measure up to our expectations of self.

The problem that you have created in your mind is that you are setting non-existent standards. In most areas of life, common sense will tell you how to behave and how not to behave, but apart from that, the rest is merely being guessed at by the whole world. You are not the only one with self-doubts, but instead of choking on them and making yourself wary of your stance on life, you should simply swallow them and not let them stop you from enjoying being you. Anxiety is a very wide spectrum within the realm of mental health, and, just like physical health, can affect the way that you interact with people and even the way you look at yourself. Think of the instance of someone who is physically ill. They don't have the patience to put up with visitors, and then feel anxious because they think they have been rude to people who care. The fact is that they are too ill to respond to normal conversation, and that's acceptable. Then look at it from a mental standpoint. If you are depressed, you may not want to talk to people, but then you kick yourself for being anti-social. Why? Is one of these illnesses less important than the other? Of course not. Anxiety can get so bad that you worry about everything, and turning that stress inward is not unusual for people who don't know how to express their thoughts outwardly.

So, what kind of behaviors would imply that you may have confidence or self-esteem problems when it comes to your day to day life? Insecurities and fears may be as follows:

☐ You may not feel that you measure up.

☐ You may worry that you haven't got what it takes.

☐ You may feel like you are a failure before you have even tried.

☐ You may not be able to face people in a confrontation.

☐ You may not be a good at arguing your point.

☐ You may allow others to walk all over you.

☐ You may not feel that you fit well into your perceived role in life.

☐ You may lack purpose.

The problem with all of these is that they can cause feelings of confusion. We have it thrown down our throats every day that we need to adhere to certain rules. Some take notice of what they see on their Facebook feed and see that as reality, while others may take their lead from the TV or the magazines that they read, but most of this insecurity comes from how comfortable you are in the skin you are in and the way that you have faced life up to this point. Bad experiences will contribute to negative self-image and anxiety. Let's examine the above points so you can see what's happening in each case.

Measuring Up

In this case, you may feel that your parents compared you with a sibling who was more successful than you or perhaps was their favorite. It's not a good start when you are compared because you go through life thinking that comparison is normal. However, no two individuals are the same, so the comparison is very unfair. If you were to look at the photos of girls of your age in magazines, some would be very pretty, while others may be fairly plain. Some will have amazing achievements in their lives, and some will have mediocre ones. The point about measuring up is that at some time in your life, you feel that you were compared, and if you carry on believing in comparisons, you will always measure your performance and be anxious about it. Instead of doing that, it's wise to understand where this came from in your thought patterns and then tell yourself that this is something you are going to stop in its tracks, using the habits detailed in the next chapter.

You Haven't Got What It Takes

This is too subjective to be true. It's a defeatist attitude, and it comes from negative thought processes and a lack of self-esteem, which both play on your emotional levels. It's not realistic, and when you are in a better frame of mind, you will find that you do indeed have what it takes and that this frame of mind is simply caused by being overwhelmed. When you learn to control that, as you will from the habits included in the next chapter, you need never be overwhelmed again. It's very much in the same category as feeling you are a failure before you even try something.

All of these defeatist attitudes are happening for a reason, and it's not the reason you may think it is. It has nothing to do with the thoughts being true. It has everything to do with anxiety and how it makes you feel. If you accept that your anxiety is fueling more anxiety and insecurity, then you can start to work toward making yourself feel more capable and deserving.

Fears are born through experience as well as expectations. We live in a period when instant gratification is pushed as the norm but is it really as viable as you think? For instance, fear comes from many areas in a woman's life, including the following:

☐ Fear of loneliness

☐ Fear of poverty

☐ Fear of pregnancy

☐ Fear of childlessness

☐ Fear of getting old

☐ Fear of our weight being out of control

We place far too many expectations on our own shoulders because of what we perceive as social norms. Fear stokes the fires of insecurity, and thus these are areas that a woman needs to be aware of so that she can protect herself from emotional harm. The strong and confident woman has none of these fears because she has learned to take life at a pace that suits her and her lifestyle. This chapter is merely intended to outline how differently women perceive things when compared to men. Men are the providers and will fight tooth and nail to provide. Women, on the other hand, are more complex, and without even being aware of it, they will think of life from the perspective of their emotional state. A woman's hormonal differences to her male counterpart are obvious, and the biggest difference will be seen in the testosterone levels, which is normally higher in men and lower in their female counterparts.

When you consider the number of people who suffer from anxiety disorders, the numbers are frightening. Women suffer more than men; statistics show that the figure for women is 23 percent higher than that of men. That isn't meant to belittle the stress experienced by men at all but is only shown to emphasize that it's quite probable that a woman will suffer from anxiety or stress at some time in their lives, particularly between the puberty and the age of 50. The symptoms of an anxiety disorder can include:

☐ Breathing difficulties

☐ Higher blood pressure

☐ Increased heart rate

☐ Panic attacks

☐ Finding difficult to concentrate for extended periods

☐ Experiencing gastric problems

☐ Finding it difficult to sleep

It all sounds pretty scary, but many of these symptoms are a byproduct of other symptoms. For example, the increased heart rate will come about because of higher blood pressure, and panic attacks may be precipitated by difficulty in sleeping or being unable to breathe correctly. The difficulty in concentration may simply be because you didn't get sufficient rest; the gastric problems may stem from the fact that because of your nervousness, you ate too quickly or didn't chew the food correctly. The point of this chapter is to let you know what's going on inside and why it causes fears, anxiety, and insecurities. The whole-body package counts, rather than one symptom simply being thought of as a unique symptom not affecting other parts of your body or its functions. The body is in harmony when you are happy and healthy, and that's important to note, especially if you suffer from one or two symptoms at a time.

Insecurities, on the other hand, are usually caused by a lack of confidence. Perhaps this has come about because you have had experiences in the past where you felt that you have failed. The hippocampus has remembered that feeling of failure and keeps reminding you of it when you attempt to do anything of a similar nature. This is where the re-education of the hippocampus becomes a necessary part of growth.

The next chapter is extensive, so you need a choose a time to read it when you can take in what's being said and use the exercises included in the chapter to try to work out solutions to your insecurities and your anxieties. When you take the actions suggested in that chapter, you will see improvements that may surprise you. It's a case of understanding what you are doing to yourself through your thought processes and then turning them around so that you no longer feel anxious about your place in the world. You are a human being with normal feelings and emotions, but you just haven't learned to use them for your betterment, rather than to make you feel less than complete. Once you do, you will find that life gets better, and you gain self-esteem and begin to like the person that you have become. So will the hippo! He doesn't like working hard on negative things, and if you can make him happy, you make yourself happy at the same time.

You have the power to remove the anxiety from your life, and when you develop the habits that are outlined in the next chapter, expect success, because each one of the habits listed has been proven to work. You will even find that Oprah Winfrey and other celebrities perform similar habits, and their lives are a testament to the efficiency of the habits you are about to introduce into your life.

Chapter Six: 8 Habits that Boost Self-Esteem

"I have learned that champions are not just born. Champions can be made when they embrace and commit to life-changing positive habits."
– Lewis Howes

Self-esteem can be boosted by taking certain actions, and this chapter is all about those boosts to your self-esteem. These take place little by little and become habitual ways of facing every new day. Habits are formed easily, although initially, you will need to work out what habits are beneficial, and this chapter will help you to embrace habits that help in self-development rather than those that shrink the importance of who you are. When you take on a new habit, try to make it something that you do daily, so that it becomes who you are rather than something you have to work at in the future. When you perform habits each day, then the hippocampus remembers these responses, and it won't be long before you are performing those habits without having to prompt yourself. I want you to watch a video made by Oprah Winfrey on the subject of Believing in Yourself. You can make such a difference in your life by changing your habits. Remember, if you repeat an action over and over again, it makes your hippocampus remember your reaction and repeat it in the future. Thus, although it may take a little bit of effort at first, when the hippocampus knows this is your priority, you will be doing all of these things on autopilot, requiring very little effort on your part. That's why these habits work and are the secret to self-esteem and happiness.

Habit Number One – Dress for Self-Confidence

There's nothing quite as frustrating as finding that the dress you saw on someone stunning doesn't suit you or do your figure any favors. It makes you feel inferior to that person in some way, but the fact is that different women have different body shapes, and it's important to get to know yours. There will be certain outfits that make you feel good about yourself, while others do nothing to boost your self-esteem. You may have trouble imagining something called "enclothed cognition," but when I explain what this means, you will get a better idea about it. When scientists wanted to find out if clothing made any difference to the self-image, they found something pretty startling. At Northwestern University, an experiment on clothing was done by introducing people to different kinds of clothing to see whether their level of concentration was affected by the clothing that they were asked to wear. The typical response by those who were asked to wear a white doctor's jacket was much more pronounced than when being asked to wear a painter's outfit. We assume that there are intelligence levels attached to different jobs and therefore perceive the doctor's job as requiring more intelligence than the painter's job. It may not be so, but it is what our perceptions tell us.

We also dress in a certain manner for different occasions. For example, when you wear your casual clothing, you are not expecting to be placed in a formal situation. Thus, wearing your jeans and sweater at home is quite normal. However, dressing is more than all of this, and the more comfortable you feel in the clothing you wear, for the situation that you have to face, the better. A smart suit for an interview is normal apparel by society norms, though some people don't seem to get that it's not just about the suit. It's about how comfortable the person in the suit is, and that starts with the underwear that you wear. If you wear a bra that is two sizes too small, simply because you don't want to admit you have put on weight, for example, you actually emphasize the lumps and bumps. Therefore, when you put on your outer garments, those bumps and lumps are visible. However, if you buy the correct size (and take the labels off if you don't want anyone to know what size you take) you smooth the lines of your clothing.

A 2014 survey of women asked what women felt made them feel the most confident, and in their answers, they included the classic black dress, high heels, and a great perfume. However, you can feel confident in colors that suit your personality as well as styles that make you feel good about the way that you look. The added perfume is simply your way of saying, "I feel good about me."

The psychology of the way that you dress says a lot about who you are and what you feel about yourself. For example, someone who perpetually hides their figure behind baggy clothing isn't making the most of themselves but is, in fact, drawing attention to themselves.

There are also body parts that will dictate what's best to wear and a woman who knows what her strong points are will dress so that those strong points are what people see. Scarves and accessories are a great way to make a dull outfit shine, and colors introduced into your wardrobe should be those that suit your skin shade and that enhance your hair color. The overall look is the thing that you are trying to create, and when you get it right, you will psychologically know that you have and feel that you can face the world without inner turmoil about your clothing or the way people look at you.

Habit Number Two: Take It to The Tribe

For a moment, think about friends that you know and trust. These are usually people who make you feel good about being who you are. The fact that you can choose your friendships is a bonus that many do not take. For example, if someone makes you feel small, why do you spend so much time being influenced by that negativity? For the sake of this exercise, write down a list of people that you know and divide them into three columns. The first column will be casual friendships, or perhaps people you know from work but don't have any real contact with them outside of the workplace. Then you have the column of people you cannot avoid. These may be family and friends of the family with whom you are not close, but who will nonetheless influence the way you feel about yourself.

The last column is the tribe. These are people you tell your secrets to. They are the folks who stand by you through thick and thin and who don't mind listening to your woes as well as sharing your victories. These are the most important influences on your self-esteem, as they make you feel good about yourself. The idea of this exercise is to weigh how much time you spend with each type of person. The second group can include people you know through your family but who are emotionally draining or friends that you once trusted but who use you. One of the least healthy types of friendship is the user, as this is a person who will make you feel that you are there to listen to them but who never listen to you. They are the people who ask favors but never return them. These are one-sided relationships that are almost toxic to your self-esteem and who make you feel like someone else's doormat.

It's vital to divide your time more beneficially so that you spend more time with your true tribe – those who love and understand you and who like you as you are. These are people who will build self-esteem and make you feel good about who you are. If you can divide your time a little more efficiently so that you get to hang out with those people more, then you will certainly increase your self-esteem. People who use you are breaking your self-esteem down, so you need to learn to say "no," even if you feel that you don't have a valid excuse. Excuses are not necessary, and although the first time is always the hardest, they will soon get the message and move on to someone else who is willing to do their bidding. The power that you gain from making your own choices will have been worth it.

Habit Number Three: Asserting Who You Are

Sometimes it is hard to say what you want to say because people with a lack of self-esteem don't feel that they can stick up for themselves when it comes to even small things like saying "No", but the fact is that you empower others when you keep saying "yes" all the time and don't have it in you to say "no." Why give away that right? There is a very good way that you can help yourself to get over this hump. If you have something more important to do, then you won't feel as bad about asserting your views to others. For example, if you do voluntary work at the local dog shelter or help out with something locally that takes up some of your time, you not only get to feel better about yourself, but you also find that you have less time in which to say "yes" to people who don't deserve your help. These are, as explained above, people who use you or take you for granted. Once in a while, it empowers you to be able to say "no, sorry, I am busy", and to simply make them sort their own problems out. Another way in which you can assert yourself is by being influenced by your real friends about what makes you look good and stop giving in to those relatives who insist on buying you awful clothing items.

Denise was very influenced by her parents and found that she couldn't make her own choices because they were always making choices for her. Then she discovered how to assert herself without offending anyone simply by telling them that she preferred to do something else, or that she preferred to wear something else. You see, though our parents are there to guide us through the initial phases of our lives, they are not our keepers. They know that eventually you will grow up and make your own decisions. When Denise understood what assertiveness could do for her self-esteem, she made changes, and they were life changing. In fact, she was quite shocked at the respect that she gained from her parents for being able to make her own decisions instead of relying so heavily upon them.

What Are You Doing When You Assert Yourself?

You are expressing opinions, and every person on earth is entitled to have an opinion. If you decide who you are going to vote for, it's recognized as your right, but it's also self-assertive. No one else knows whose name you put a cross next to, so in effect, you are making up your own mind. You may be influenced by others and have been brought up to believe certain things, but if you make your mind up as to which candidate is best because you understand what they stand for, and choose them, then this is self-assertion. Under the law, you are not answerable to anyone as to whom you chose to vote for. However, take it outside of the polling booth, and you start to worry about offending people, or you start to worry about whether you've got what it takes to make decisions. Some people grow up and get married still lacking assertion skills, and will let their partners make all of the decisions, but that's never a good way to go because self-assertion says, "Hey, there's two people in this relationship and both of us count." It makes you count for something. It doesn't mean being contrary for the sake of it. What it does mean is that if you have a point of view, you are entitled to express it.

What you are doing to yourself is pretty amazing. You are reinforcing who you are, and thus it's a little like affirmations. Each time you decide on your own, you are reinforcing the fact that you are capable of making decisions. You may make mistakes from time to time, but that's human too, and if you learn to laugh at those mistakes –if they aren't too grave– or learn from them for the future –if they are important– then your assertion isn't wasted. However, never think that self-assertion is rudeness or that it's something you are not entitled to. You do it every day without even knowing it. Let's show you some examples:

☐ I must get out of bed

☐ I am going to wear a red dress today

☐ I am going to have eggs for breakfast

☐ I am going to walk to work today because it's sunny

Every action you take in your day is an assertion in one way or another, and self-assertion is the difference between someone making you get out of bed, someone insisting that you wear the blue dress when you planned to wear the red one, someone making you have toast instead of eggs for breakfast, or someone insisting that you drive to work on that sunny day. Do you see how it works? You put yourself into the driving seat of your life by making assertions, and each time you do, you build a little more solid foundation for who you are and who you will become. Each time you let others assert things that rule your life, you give them the power instead and start to shrink back from life – almost like living in the shadows.

Step out of the shadows of your life and start making decisions about what's going to happen today, and you start to feel like a whole human being instead of having your life dictated to you by other people. Of course, in the work environment, you have to do what your boss tells you, but imagine that feeling of being able to explain to your boss a quicker way of doing mundane tasks, or being able to show your boss that you know more than he gives you credit for. These all help you in the bid to assert who you are. Similarly, in an interview for a job, change your mindset. Ask yourself how much you want the job and how valuable you know that you are. Often when you are selling yourself in a situation like this, it pays to be convinced that you have a lot to offer, rather than to shrink into a corner not knowing what to say. Be bold in your life and learn that assertion is merely about expressing an opinion, and you won't go far wrong.

Look at the cases above, where it becomes apparent that you were able to make up your mind about things like getting out of bed, etc. Now, look at other choices in the same way. If you go to dinner with friends and you don't want to eat French fries, tell them you are on a restricted diet. It's not inconvenient, and you are entitled to assert yourself. If someone offers you coffee and you prefer tea, then say so. A little bit of assertion every day will help you to become more confident and improve your self-esteem, but they don't have to be major things. As you go through this exercise, write down what you achieved in each day for the next seven days by speaking your mind instead of just making do. You have a voice, and now is the time to start to exercise it.

Habit Number Four: Using Affirmations

I know you have probably laughed about the idea of telling yourself you are beautiful every time that you look in the mirror, or that this will make you beautiful. However, if you look seriously into the subject of affirmations and also understand about how the brain works, it's easy to see a pattern. Feed your mind negative statements, and all that you attract into your life is negativity. You feel bad about being you. You lose confidence and lack self-esteem, and all of this negative feedback is adding to the bleakness of your life. It follows quite logically that if you can reframe the things that you say to yourself into positive statements – or affirmations – then the opposite happens. Let's look at some of the things you are likely to say to yourself regularly:

☐ I can't do this

☐ I can't wear something like that

☐ I look fat

☐ I won't get the job

☐ I am out of my league

The problem here is that the longer you repeat this to the hippocampus, the more it believes it, and you are powering up the negativity so that your own negativity hits your confidence levels. However, if you reframe everything and look at every aspect of your life as an opportunity rather than a dread, you will find yourself capable of doing much more than you originally gave yourself credit for. Let's look at some positive affirmations that may help you to start your day in the right way.

☐ The sun is shining, and I am starting my day off with optimism

☐ Even the clouds have a silver lining, and thing will get better today

☐ I love getting up early and enjoying a relaxing breakfast

☐ I love taking care of myself and enjoying my walking hours

All of these are positive statements that give you a little bit of a buzz to start your day. Energy is at its highest in the morning, but if you start the day with negativity, the level of negativity is also high, and that will hold you back from enjoying your life. The kind of affirmations that work is not the "I could...." Affirmations, because the "I am" affirmations are more powerful. Let me give you a demonstration of someone who believed that he would win the lottery. He was so convinced that he would win that he started to think positively, similarly to someone who already had the money. His logic was not flawed. If you want to be rich, you can't think like a poor man. His affirmations included things like:

☐ I know how to manage my money

☐ I know how to attract money toward me

These are just money-oriented, and in your case, we want to create realistic affirmations that use all of your positive attributes to give you more confidence. They must have a certain element of truth, and you need to change your approach each day toward thinking of all the nice things about yourself, rather than dwelling on what you see as weak points. There is absolutely nothing wrong with celebrating who you are or even feeling smug sometimes about the little things that you achieve. Start giving yourself more goals that you can achieve and then use affirmations to congratulate yourself, and soon you will find that affirmations come naturally to you. For instance, you always leave the kitchen a mess in the morning. Change tack. Put away the dishes and then tell yourself, "I am tidy and clean and can organize my life." Then when you have a habit of being late to meetings, turn up early. Tell yourself, "I am always prepared for the things I need to do." Although you may take a little convincing at the start, if you get into the habit of doing this with all of the tasks you do each day, you drown out the negative voice and fill your mind with positivity about who you are and what you represent. Affirmations can be used in all areas of your life. For example, whenever you feel positive about something, note it mentally and tell yourself you are good at that thing, because the affirmations you make from these feel-good moments are worth it and you are basing them on actual fact, so you can't question whether they are true or not. Affirmations are not about intentions. They are about who you are and what you are and should always be positive and reinforcing so that you see improvements in your ability to mix with different kinds of people as well as noting an improvement in the way that you view yourself.

☐ I am great with kids and love animals

☐ I have a heart filled with love for others

☐ I am thoughtful and kind

☐ I am a person who succeeds

☐ My friends like me

Of course, there are many more that you can add to it. After cooking a successful meal, you may want to add "I am a great cook," and this may help you to have less doubt when you have to cook for the company. All of these things are positive notions that you repeat to yourself so that they become your way of thinking. Think success; be successful. It works because your hippocampus will eventually pull out all of these affirmations and see them as being something worth holding onto so that you can approach new situations from a more positive perspective.

Habit Number Five: Adopt a Goddess Mindset

You may be asking yourself what kind of nonsense this is but bear me out because you must listen to me. The Goddess Mindset is something that is inherently a part of being a woman. As you grow up, it's there waiting for you to take advantage of it, and during your teens, you probably have seen it from time to time, when you look in the mirror and feel really good about who you are. Little by little, life tends to chip away at it and make you question your values. That's when the Goddess Mindset gets crushed, and women become less than they ever intended to be. In fact, they lose themselves in the process.

Let's take this back to basics. Do you remember when you were a little girl and perhaps thought of yourself as a princess? No? Well, as far back as that, that little Goddess inside you was telling you who you were, and you instantly became that person. The princess was just a small part of it. The girl who made a wonderful cake at school may have thought of herself as the next trend in cooking, or the girl who sang could imagine herself as the next Madonna. However, the

Goddess mindset develops or disintegrates, depending upon your image of who you are. The first line of questioning to ascertain whether you have the Goddess Mindset is:

☐ Do you trust yourself?

☐ Do you believe in yourself?

☐ Are you the best person you think you can be?

If you have any doubts about any of these questions, then you need to work on gaining that knowledge of yourself that allows you to answer them in the affirmative. The trust issue is easy. If you promise something, do you follow through? If you say you will help a friend, do you do it? Issues such as false promises may come from things such as wanting to slim or wanting to give up cigarettes, but these are temporary situations rather than core values. Core values that make up the inner Goddess mindset are those that say that you know who you are and like who you are. You believe in yourself, and you see yourself at your best at this moment in time. It's not about the fancy dress you wear. It's about how you feel in the skin you are in. Some wonderful videos on YouTube cover this subject, and from people you may not identify as Goddesses. They may not be the most beautiful women. They may not be all style and show, but the one thing that these women have in common is that they truly believe they are the best that they can be and will go on improving on that so that they remain that way rather than getting complacent in their approach to life.

There are two methods of getting your Goddess Mindset. One is to remind yourself of all the nice things that you do in life and to build upon this foundation, and the other is distinctly different; instead of thinking outside of your own needs, to the needs of others, you need to stop making comparisons of yourself with other people's expectations of you. When push comes to shove, all that matters is that you spend time with people YOU approve of, rather than seeking approval from others or taking notice of what other people think about you. Their thoughts are of small significance to your life unless you let them become significant, and that's where the Goddess mindset comes into play. I am who I am, but can other people around me measure up? It's a case of reverse psychology. For example, when you go out on a date, stop worrying about how you will appear to the person you are dating. Start to concentrate your attention on questions such as "Will he live up to expectations? Will he amuse me? Will he be funny and quirky?" You are not judging. What you are doing is taking the focus away from who you are and working out if people fit into your life. If they don't, then they have no right to be there.

I have mentioned hanging out with your crowd or your tribe, but it doesn't just mean those people who make you happy. It also means those people who will, of course, give you the job, those people who will be positive in their approach, and certainly those people who recognize you for the goddess that you are.

Let the goddess come out to play sometimes. Be that Princess, be that special someone because when you stop letting yourself enjoy the liberation of just being you, you start to measure yourself, and that helps no one. You start to worry about what you have to give instead of being rightly worried about who you want in your life and who will help you to retain that goddess. If someone stifles your creativity, for example, should you live with it? Or should you make a point of allowing your creativity to come out in another way? You have to cater to the goddess, or you will lose her, and many women give up the right to be a goddess when they stop pleasing themselves and start to depend upon pleasing others.

Habit Number Six: Meditation

A lot of women that I work with don't really know the meaning of meditation and don't like the idea because it's beyond the scope of their knowledge. However, when they introduce it and practice it daily, I have them running to me with stories about how free they feel and how capable of expressing themselves they have become. Their confidence soars. Their ability to mix with people is extraordinary, and their acceptance of self is undeniable. You may not know it, but that part of the woman's brain that deals with emotions needs to be left to its own devices sometimes. The rush of thoughts and the amount of multi-tasking that we subject it to isn't what it was designed for.

I told you before about the hippocampus – our friend who registers our important actions and memories. The hippocampus changes new habits and incorporates them into the day-to-day activities that you do, so it's a very good thing to feed the hippo with all of the right kinds of food. Let me show you what happens when you meditate:

Your blood pressure goes down – That's going to stop you from having panic attacks and will enable you to be more in control of your life.

Your heart rate slows – This is going to benefit heart health and longevity.

Your mind is emptied of clutter – This is a wonderful side effect of meditation because it helps you to have a clear mind and see things for what they really are without blowing everything up into a panic. If you lack confidence, you will gain it through meditation because you are no longer stuffing your mind full of negativity.

You will learn not to judge people or situations – Have you ever had a conversation with someone, thought about what they said, and then exaggerated it so much that you have all kinds of ideas about the conversation that make it a mental burden to you? People, especially those who lack self-esteem, read things into what others say. They ask themselves things like:

☐ Does he really like me, or is he just being polite?

☐ Is she trying to make me look good with that dress or trying to make a fool of me?

☐ Does that color really suit me, or were people just being polite?

☐ Does this hairstyle really look good, or are people just being kind?

These are thoughts that would be classed by people who meditate as being the "monkey mind." It's the part of you that has conversations with itself and who makes mountains out of molehills. Well, meditation quietens down that part of the mind so that you are not afraid of silence, not afraid of being alone, and certainly not afraid of letting nature help you to heal. Meditation declutters all of the boxes of thoughts that you have been tossing around in your head and seals those boxes so that you can think only about *now*, and quite frankly, that's the only time that really matters. If you made a mistake in the past, you can't undo it. You can apologize if you think you hurt someone, but you can't change what you did. It's over, and it's done with, and with meditation, you learn to catch up with yourself and be here and now, rather than in the land of regrets and remorse. Both of those words are negative and will not help confidence at all. Mistakes are mistakes, and the only way to get past them is to learn from them; meditation clears your mind sufficiently to do that.

So, What's Special About Meditation?

It means sitting in a quiet place in a certain pose so that energy can run through you as you breathe. You concentrate on the breathing method that is given to you for a purpose. It's not to avoid thoughts. It is simply to show you that you can think of things that are more productive and not prioritize your emotional problems and dramas. It helps you to let your body heal you, rather than trying to do this with your conscious thoughts. The one benefit that I have found from meditation –which is why I teach women to do this daily– is that you feel refreshed and at peace with the world, instead of always being at odds with it. You are more creative, and you also learn what's happening inside your body when you breathe, and have a lot more respect for your body. It makes you feel at one with the world, and when that happens, you can use it during your day for short moments, simply to remind yourself of what YOU are all about, rather than letting the world around you twist who you are into someone with self-esteem issues and lack of confidence. All of the negative thoughts that you have come from inside your head and meditation helps you to put those aside and to realize that your true potential lies in knowing yourself and loving who you are.

So, What Does Happen in the Body When You Meditate?

You have something inside you called the sympathetic nervous system. This does many jobs within the body, such as controlling temperatures or making sure that the right amount of oxygen is pumped to all the right places. When you breathe in the way that you are taught for meditation, you help to regulate what's happening in your body. You awaken your intuition, that little voice that tells you what's good for you and what's not, the one that you may not have been listening to for a while. Altogether, the sympathetic nervous system is put into overdrive and works more efficiently so that you feel better, but you also need to feed yourself with good nourishing food and make sure that you drink sufficient water and get enough sleep. All of these body issues get in the way of your happiness if they are neglected. Meditation pulls you back into the positive loop so that you know which direction your life is going in and are happier with who you are and what life offers you.

Many of the physical symptoms that women feel throughout their lives are dictated by the release of hormones within the body. Your monthly venture into womanhood is part of this process, but some women go through an awful time while others sail through. Meditation helps you to balance pain and helps the brain to know which hormones to release to make you feel good about life. That solid foundation for your life is brought about by a twenty-minute-a-day habit of meditating, so it's not a huge price to pay. It is such an enormous subject that I have decided to devote the next part of this chapter to it to do it justice. I do hope that you will enjoy what you read and will be able to use it in your life.

How to Meditate

The first thing that you need to decide is where you can meditate. It should be a place where you will not be disturbed and where you feel comfortable; if you set up an area in which to meditate, it tends to enthuse you, and you are investing yourself into the habit. You may need a yoga mat and a supportive cushion, but if you have limited mobility you can use a specific chair, which should be a hard chair with a straight back. However, you can make the whole experience of meditation a little more motivating by adding things that you find inspirational around your chosen area, such as candles or a Buddha statue or a few favorite plants. When you meditate, you are not worshipping at all, so it has no bearing on what religion you follow. You simply use the Buddha statue or whatever you choose for inspiration. It could even be a photo of someone dear to you or a vase of flowers.

The seating position for meditation, if you use a cushion, is to sit with your back straight and then bend the knees and cross the ankles. Make sure that you are centered by swaying right and left until you are sure you are comfortable. Then place your hands on your lap with the palms facing upward and one hand cupping the other. Touch your thumbs together. If you are using a chair, sit with your back straight, and do not be tempted to lean back. Place your feet flat on the floor. You can also place your hands on your lap, as in the cushion position.

Make sure that you have comfortable clothes that are not going to distract you by chafing or binding. That's very important because there's nothing like a tight waistband to take your mind off meditation. Now, start to breathe, in through the nostrils to the count of 8, and then out to the count of 10. It's not like your normal breathing, which is relatively shallow. In the case of meditation, it's purposeful breathing, and the idea is that you sink into this moment in the breath, and that means concentrating solely on what's happening to your body as you breathe, rather than letting external thoughts get into the way. You need to continue to do this until you feel that the pattern of breathing is taking on a rhythm. Then, continuing to breathe in and breathe out, at the end of each cycle of inhalation and exhalation, you count one, then two, then three, etc.

The idea of meditation is clearing the mind, so if you get any thoughts that come to your mind while you are meditating, you simply let them go. Do not judge them, and do not let them form a chain of thoughts in your mind. Just let them go. They may be things that you need to deal with at a later time, but now is not the time to think about them. Let go and breathe. If you need to concentrate on anything, think about the air going down into your body and the way it leaves the body, and be aware of movements within your body that happen while you are breathing. You are in this moment, and traveling in your mind to other moments is what you are trying not to do. In fact, you are not really even trying. You are simply letting go and letting yourself be at this moment in time. Keep this up for around 20 minutes each morning when you get up and over the next week or so, you will begin to notice a difference in your approach to life. Don't expect sudden changes as there won't be any. Just go with the flow, and if thoughts come to your head, don't kick yourself for them. It's a natural progression, and learning to let go is the hardest part, but it doesn't require concentration. When you concentrate on something, you take away the spontaneity of it, so just go with the flow and allow yourself to breathe and count, breathe and count. Remember what I said about your blood pressure and heart rate? These will go down during meditation, so you must not get up quickly when you think that you have finished. Instead of doing this, it's a good idea to have a journal next to you so that you can record what you felt at the end of a meditation session and make notes on how you think you can improve that meditation the next time around. Perhaps some things distracted you during the meditation, and you can move them for next time so that you don't experience that same irritation again.

There are other ways to meditate that may be helpful to you. If you feel that your eyes need something to look at while you meditate, then guided meditation is a good way to go. In this case, you will choose something to concentrate your eyes on while you breathe, and this can be the flame of a candle or a statue or even a photograph of someone who inspires you. However, if you have never meditated before, I suggest that meditation with the eyes closed is a lot easier because you take away the potential of distraction. Meditation doesn't work magic that you can notice straight away. It clears the mind so that you can make better decisions. It makes the liaison between the mind and body more pronounced so that you care more about your place in the world and take action to make yourself healthier and happier. It's a great foundation upon which to build yourself because you let go of all of the things that do not form parts of that moment, such as past hurts or future worries.

You may not know it, but you can use meditation anywhere. Simply close your eyes and breathe and be oblivious to what's happening around you. It's useful before a stressful meeting or when you are going for an interview. It helps to sharpen your mind and can be used to calm down the stresses and strains that life imposes upon you. Are you meeting someone new for the first time? Breathe in and out as you do with meditation before meeting them, and you are likely to be less nervous. Worried about taking some exams? Breathe in and out and close your eyes for a moment before entering the exam room. You have the necessary skills to pass those exams. What detracts from them is the nervousness that your mind imposes on yourself, and meditation helps to set the balance right. Meditation helps you in so many areas of your life, and once you learn to take it with you through your life, you take that sense of calm with you and let go of your anxieties forever. Being this aware of your state of mind helps you to be stronger so that anxieties have the opposite effect on you and simply make you more convinced that there are always solutions.

Habit Number Seven: Do What You Love ANYWAY

Each day when you get out of bed, you surround yourself with familiarity. You get used to doing certain things and having certain habits, but what if I told you that it's okay to let go and let the inner child out sometimes? You would probably laugh it off and not even attempt it, but it is worth it, and soon you will know why. People hold themselves back because they believe that society expects them to behave in a certain way, and yes, to a degree, politeness is expected, and being decent to others is common sense, but what about the rest of it? Are you typecast? If you are overweight, for example, would you avoid going to the gym? If you are skinny, would you avoid the beach because you feel you will be criticized? Often people with self-esteem issues make those issues larger than life by giving up on things that they love doing, but that they feel self-conscious about doing. Ellen loved to act but was always typecast into roles that were minor because the mistress at her school did not believe her body fit the roles that Ellen wanted. We let ourselves down when we stop doing something we love simply because society expects us to take a back seat.

To do what you love to do, you have to know what it is that you perceive as being something you really would love to do. It's no good saying that life won't let you do things and being vague about it, so you need to take the following steps, so you can do the things you love:

Step One: Know What You Want to Do

There's nothing wrong with writing into a journal the things that you want to do in your life. No one is going to live your life for you, and if you love doing these things, no one has the right to stop you. For example, Sara wanted to make patchwork quilts, but she never really gave herself the time to do it. She got around this by allowing herself a small amount of time each day to quilt and gradually got more proficient, ending up several years later giving demonstrations of quilting and even having her own exhibition. If you can't pinpoint the things that you want to do, you will never achieve them, so work out your bucket list of things you want to do, even if these are tiny things that bring you joy and laughter. Helen wanted to jump in a puddle. She had lived in the city most of her life and had seen kids doing this in the country and had this vision of joy in her mind about doing it and not caring about getting wet. She waited, but she kept it on her bucket list and actually did it, and that feeling gave her new confidence that all of her goals, no matter how big or small, were possibilities rather than simply dreams.

Step Two: Find Out What Obstacles are Getting in Your Way

For this step, you need to look realistically at what's stopping you from doing those things that you see yourself doing to give yourself joy. If it's money, you can save and work toward accruing a nest egg. If it's a case of feeling you don't have a voice, give yourself one. If you feel that life is not giving you time, make that time. You have to work out what's stopping you and then work on taking away those obstacles because you are the only one who can.

Step Three: Live the Life You Imagined and Start Today

We can all close our eyes and imagine what will bring joy into our lives, but if you find things that truly make you feel good, then you need to start to make those things happen. Don't let others stop you. Don't let your shyness or your self-esteem issues get in the way because it's only you who sees those negative thoughts, and others around you are struggling just as much as you are to get their voices heard. Yet, every day we read stories of women who have started doing what they love and making their lives fulfilled and enjoyable. You can, too. You need to create the ideal picture of who you are rather than worry about how you are perceived. Be the best person that you can be to fit in with the joys you want to encompass in your life.

Habit Number Eight: Share your Story

How many women do you imagine feeling the way that you do? Perhaps there are millions, because looking at the state of mental health all over the world, we know that the numbers of illnesses that are related to self-esteem and self-doubt are on the rise. One of the most inspirational websites I ever read was a blog written by a woman who suffered from self-esteem issues. She wasn't afraid to tell her story, and the inspiration that it gave to many women all over the world was amazing. She started out very unsure of herself, but as her story unfolded, so did the comments from other women who had suffered similar self-esteem issues who no longer felt that they were alone and who were able to build each other up through mutual support by showing total honesty about their fears in life and what they had done to overcome them.

Although you may not feel like a leader at this stage, the feedback that you get from blogs is very sensitive; people like you don't get slammed for being who they are. Women all over the world are looking for solutions to their problems. They are not looking for problems, and the comment section on each page of your personal blog can be inspirational and help you to see that you do not lack in any way at all. Being able to express yourself in words is helpful from a therapeutic point of view as well, and many women have used this platform to make others aware of what it feels like to be lacking in confidence and self-esteem. Did you know that writing your life story can be liberating? It helps with freeing all of those negative thoughts so that you don't have to relive them every day. You are letting them out onto the page, and psychologically this can be extremely powerful in the search for self-esteem.

If you decide to go this route, then make sure that you have a good audience, by learning all about keywords because it is these words that lead people to your blog. Many blog sites have helpful forums to tell you how to draw attention to your blog and place it in the right category so that the right people see it. You can also link it to a Facebook account and find many readers through your social networking sites.

If you are a little wary of letting friends and family know about how you feel, then create a Facebook account just for this purpose and befriend others who may be interested in reading a woman's story; you will be surprised how many are. It's a boost to your self-esteem, and if you keep your stories up to date and interesting, you really can help others by helping yourself.

The habits that have been included in this section are all healthy habits that you can make into a part of your everyday life. When you embrace these habits, you will find that you are more creative, happier, more well-accepted and that your self-esteem will be boosted by the results that you get. I have seen so many women turn their lives around simply by adopting these habits and making themselves surer of their footing in the world. The work that you put into learning these habits will make a true difference to the way that people react toward you and increase your acceptance of the fact that everyone has different choices that are right for them. Just because yours seem a little different doesn't make them wrong. It merely means that you are exercising your individuality, and that's going to help you to like who you are and accept yourself.

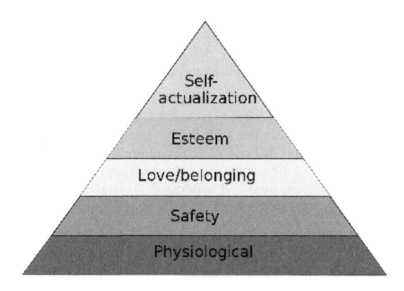

Self-esteem is a great asset to have on your side. It means self-acceptance, and it also means recognizing when you shine and when your halo needs a little more polish. You are a wonderful human being but have let life cut you down to size. Now it's time to fight back and show the world that your stature is complete and that you are happy to be in your own skin. When you do, the law of attraction will work in your favor. I am not sure if you are familiar with the law of attraction, but positive people are magnets for other positive people, while misery only encourages abusive relationships and unhappy people. When you learn what your talents are, celebrate them. Make small goals for yourself and celebrate your successes. Your thoughts dictate to a very large extent how you perceive yourself and your daily meditation will help to keep those in check.

Chapter Seven: Why Self-Care is Important

"Follow your heart, listen to your inner voice, stop caring about what others think." –Roy T. Bennett

A long time ago, a psychologist named Maslow made a chart of all of the things that you need in your life in order to feel happy. It was a very clever chart made in the '40s but is still relevant today. I am going to show you the different levels of that chart and explain to you why each of them is relevant to happiness and self-fulfillment.

The elements that make up this chart are fairly obvious ones, but it may not be as obvious why these needs are important. The first line is physiological needs. That's the food that you eat and the water that you drink, as well as the shelter you need and the feeling of wellbeing that is brought about by getting enough sleep and satisfying your bodily needs for rest, vitamins and minerals from foods, and sufficient exercise. These are all bodily needs.

The safety aspect of the chart relates to how safe you are in your home, how secure you feel with people that you know, and if you can mix socially with others without too much problem, then that part of the psyche is looked after. A woman who stays at home and mixes with no one isn't doing herself any favors, because she is introducing a lack of safety into her life. There's no one to care about her. There's no one to check in and see if she is okay, and that human contact forms part and parcel of the safety net that we put around our lives.

Love and belonging come next, and these are very important aspects of being happy. They start with the way that you feel about yourself and extend to the way that you feel about others, and how they feel about you. When you take care of your needs for love, you give, but you also allow yourself to take, so that this giving and taking is in equal proportions. You get joy from giving a friend a birthday gift or going to the movies with a friend, and you can share who you are with trusted people who trust you in return. The aspect here that affects people who have self-esteem issues is that they tend to put other peoples' needs before their own. If you are incomplete, how do you expect to attract complete and wholesome people into your tribe? The fact is that you need to be happy to spend time alone as well as being happy to share it, and self-love and appreciation come into this category. When you learn to love yourself, you open the doors to real love shown by others toward you. You make yourself worth loving. Is it worth loving someone who cannot love herself? You already know the answer to that one, so self-care is extremely important, and leaving yourself to last was never the right way to do things. Sometimes, you have to put other people's needs first, but certainly not as a general rule in life.

So how does esteem come into the picture? Well, this is all about what you think of yourself and the image that you portray to others. It is all about having the right boundaries and respecting the boundaries of others. When you have self-esteem, people know where they stand with you and are more likely to trust you as you show them that you trust yourself. Self-care allows you to show the world that you do care for yourself, and you can see many examples of this in a shopping mall simply by looking around you. The perceived emotional stature of people depends upon their comportment and the way that they interact with others, but also can be seen in the way that they look after themselves.

You can never be the best person you are capable of being when you don't look after yourself. Thus, the care that you give to yourself comes out in many ways. Now let's look at some of the different categories and see why they are so important to self-actualization.

The Food That You Eat

If you are always feeding yourself food that is not nourishing, your hair suffers, your skin suffers, and you are likely to gain weight. Weight gain will ultimately give you other health problems even if these are just digestive problems for the time being. Quite often, the way that you look after your body on the inside is reflected on the outside. People who eat too much grease, for example, may have skin problems and may even find that they are putting on weight in all the wrong places. If you make the most of eating and drinking the right things, you give your body a head start; your energy levels increase, and you feel healthier and happier.

The other important element of eating and drinking is taking in sufficient water, because the water within the body needs to be replenished. If you are always drinking coffee, it's a diuretic, which means that you will lose more water through your urine. Thus, drinking glasses of plain water regularly will help to make you feel wonderful. It helps your body to send that liquid refreshment to all the right parts of your body so that you don't suffer from cramps when you are overactive or underactive. Water really is an important part of the diet.

Allowing Yourself Enough Sleep

In this day and age, many women take their phones or tablets to bed and while away the time looking at their emails and updates on their Facebook pages. The problem with this at night is that you are not allowing your mind to switch off. Other things that can keep you awake at night are:

- A bedroom that is not sufficiently aired

- A bedroom with too much heat

- An uncomfortable mattress

- Sheets that are not fresh and welcoming

- A busy mind after watching action TV too late

- Worries from the day

You need to start thinking of your bedroom as a peaceful haven where sleep happens, and prepare yourself for sleep by relaxing a little after you switch off the TV. A good book may help, and leaving your technology out of the bedroom will do wonders for your eyesight. When you get into bed, try to relax. If you can't, and you are worried about things, try to meditate yourself to sleep. It works well, as does doing a body scan. This is where you breathe in the same way that you do when you meditate but concentrate on different areas of the body, starting with the toes and working your way up through all of your body parts. Focus on your toes; tense them, and then relax them, and see how good they feel relaxed in this manner. Move onto the next part of your body and do the same until your mind is sleepy, and you can get a good night's sleep.

The Way You Present Yourself to the World

This can have a lot to do with self-esteem and self-actualization. Take care of your skin by removing make-up at night. Make sure that your hair is regularly washed and treat yourself to a great conditioner now and again. If you have dyed hair, get it done regularly so that it doesn't look as if you don't care about your looks. Others always notice the way that you look after yourself. For example, if you don't clean your teeth regularly, you may have bad breath, or if you don't wash your face every day, perhaps you greet the world with sleepy eyes.

Look at yourself in the mirror often and especially when you are about to step out into the world. Check how you look. Approve of how you look because if you approve, then it's likely that the world is going to approve as well. Are you wearing clothes that are suited to the event? For example, your work clothes should show that you take care of yourself because they are a reflection of the company that you work for. If you want a managerial job, then you won't get it by not looking the part. Companies want their employees to show the world what the company standards are, so you must look your best for whatever job you do.

Similarly, working in a farm environment, you would hardly be welcome if you turned up in high heels and a short skirt. Practical jobs require practical clothing and reflect the thought that you put into what you are going to be doing. Dressing for a party is pretty safe if you check with the host(s) or other attendees as to what kind of dress is appropriate. These extra checks are worthwhile because when you know how you are expected to dress, you tend to look the part, rather than being unprepared and dressing inappropriately.

The Effect of Colors

You may not be aware of it, but if you dress in colors that are "happy" colors, you are likely to feel more optimistic toward the world, and if that helps your mental state, then it's worth trying when you are considering what to wear for the day.

Taking Care of Your Posture

In the old days, you would be encouraged by your parents to sit up straight. You would perhaps be encouraged to cross a room with a book on your head. The point of these exercises was to help you to grow strong and grow upright. The problems that you get from slouching can play on your mind, but they can also do more than that. They alter your body image to others. As you have learned about how to use posture when you are meditating, it's also a good idea to make sure that your body is comfortable rather than slouched as this can affect your health as well as the image you put forward to others.

The other element regarding your posture is the fact that you have energy centers throughout your spine, and if the energy flow is interrupted, you will find that you suffer as a consequence. It may be that you suffer aches and pains when you are worried about things, and a lot of this may be in the neck and shoulders area. Thus, it's vital to make sure that you keep this part of your body straight as much as you can. It will save you a lot of problems later.

What Self-Care Does to Your Esteem Levels

Throughout my work with women, I have found that self-care is the first step toward getting your self-esteem back. Looking after your body, confidently presenting yourself, and knowing that you are doing the best that you can for your health makes you feel good inside. You are much more likely to be loveable, but you are also more likely to love yourself when you practice ongoing care of the person that you have become. Nothing makes you feel greater than having a new hairstyle or managing a move in yoga that you never managed before, and the message that you are sending to your body is no longer one of neglect. It's telling the body to work as it's intended to work, with you in the driving seat.

Chapter Eight: Self-Love – 4 Paths to Self-Love

"You yourself, as much as anybody in the entire universe, deserve your love and affection" – Sharon Salzberg

Before I go further on this subject, I want you to understand something. No one on this earth has more control over the way that your life pans out than you. You may argue that you had a dreadful childhood. You may argue that you have been through some horrendous experiences in life, but so have millions of other women and there's nothing particularly special about any one of them except the way that they handled those situations and came out on the other side knowing that ultimately, they were responsible for their own happiness. Drop the concept that you need someone else because you are incomplete. You will always be incomplete if you think in this way. However, if you take time out and stop looking, you will find that all the strength that you need in your life is there inside you, and you just need to know how to access it.

Path One – Accepting the Now

I was once unfortunate enough to be at the bedside of a lady who was dying. All of her life, she carried the weight of her past with her. It didn't matter what you told her, she always came back to the past and never really started to see beyond that until it was too late, and she was filled with regret at all of the years she had wasted in retrospection. I don't want that to happen to anyone who reads this book, and if I have anything to do with it, you won't need to go there. The first step toward self-love is accepting yourself at this moment in time, and although it sounds simple, many people in this world refuse to do that and carry on having self-esteem issues, when it's so easy to step into this moment and tell yourself that you are not a product of anything that anyone else has done to you, or of the sins that have happened in your past. You are now, and every moment of your life counts. Start to pull yourself back into this moment because that's all there is, and it can be a moment filled with misery or it can be a moment filled with the joy of being alive. Look at nature to help you. Be inspired by it. Watch the spider as he makes his web, or the flowers pop their heads up in spring to let you know that another year lies ahead. Be aware of the world around you and your part in it because that's where happiness lies, and that's where self-esteem starts.

Path Two: Believing in What You Want Out of Your Life

I talk to a lot of people about what they want, and instead of looking inside themselves for true wishes and dreams, they tend to look at material things. They also have a little voice inside them that tells them that they are never going to achieve their dreams, and this is self-defeating. You have to draw up a plan of what you want in your life, and instead of telling yourself that you can't have it, tell yourself that you already have it but that it's simply not accessible at this moment. You have to change the mindset because if you work against yourself, you are never going to love who you are. See yourself as confident and happy, and let that happiness happen. See yourself as wanting to live in a big house and keep on believing that it will happen because the moment you stop believing, you cut off your dreams and start to become very unhappy about who you are, and that's not fair to your inner self. Let yourself dream. Let your dreams be as specific as possible and believe wholeheartedly in them. It gives you a personal stand upon which to feel that you deserve the life you crave, and indeed you do, and it's only by not loving who you are that you stand back and watch others succeed and see yourself fail because you don't believe you deserve a life like theirs. You do. Everyone does.

Path Three: Acceptance

When you are a kid, it's hard to accept that the neighbor's kid has a new bike and you don't. As you grow older, you find that life isn't as simplistic as that. Perhaps the kids who had "everything" didn't actually have much. Their parents were too busy working to provide them with material things so that when it came to love and family, they weren't around much. There are always two ways of looking at everything, and when you accept who you are and where you are in life, you get to realize life is a one-way street. You are not practicing; this isn't a dry run that you can waste on self-indulgence being unhappy about who you have become. However, when you accept who you are, you find happiness within yourself that helps you to love and respect yourself for who you are. You are attracted to people who accept themselves and make good friendships that last a lifetime. Why? Because people who think like this don't look for all the regrets in their lives. They are too busy living in the moment and enjoying it.

Path Four: Use Your Losses to Become Emotionally Stronger

When you feel that you will crumble at the end of a bad relationship, the truth of the matter is that you won't crumble. You may feel bad, but you make yourself feel a whole lot worse if you throw blame into the equation. Self-blame, the blame for your partner, these are all excuses not to move on. When Kelly was told that her husband, Mark, had been killed in action, her world stopped turning for a short while, but as she stood beside his grave, looking on as the coffin was lowered into the ground, she felt a swell of love inside her that she hadn't noticed before. He had loved her. They had completed years and years of marriage and had a child that would grow up and become someone her father would be proud of. Yes, there was the anger, the regret, the unhappiness of loss, and the natural grief process, but what woke Kelly up was the fact that every day of her life with Mark, he had made her feel like she deserved life, and she did. She worked hard, she made a small humble house into a home, and these had been the best years of her life so far. What she needed to do was continue to be emotionally strong and happy inside her heart, so she used the loss as a steppingstone that helped her to help others – not because she wanted any kind of status, but simply because she could. She had learned through loss to be more compassionate in life, to be humble, and to give whatever she could to the moment that she was in. She also saw other people who, like her, had lost partners but who were not coping as well as she was, and she helped them to rebuild their lives.

No matter how badly off you are or how you believe that life has mistreated you up until this moment in time, those lessons should be clues as to how to make your life count for more than the hurt other people foisted on you; you are not a victim. You might have been in the past, but as long as you carry the victim mentality with you, you will remain one when in fact you can step out of that shell any time that you want to and use those experiences of your life to let others know that it's okay to have bad experiences, as long as you can get to the other side of them with self-love intact. Kelly started to work with other people who were feeling the same needs as hers, and through that work realized that she was worthy of the love that Mark had given her during his life, and in loving herself honored his memory in her own way.

Step Five: Forgive Others and Forgive Yourself

You are a human being, and regardless of your religion, agnosticism, or atheism, you should have learned by now that mankind is not perfect. Mistakes get made, and so many people use blame as an excuse not to move on. If you blame yourself for your misfortunes in life, you never actually get past them because you see yourself as defective. That self-image goes with you for the rest of your life unless you are prepared to forgive and forget. If you blame yourself for something, move on; forgive yourself, because forgiveness heals the scars and helps you to start over without always thinking negative thoughts about who you are. If you have had problems forgiving others, let go. It doesn't take a lot of imagination to see what this hatred or what this blame does to you; it makes you bitter. It cuts into who you are and takes away your self-esteem. Angry people don't like themselves much, so let go of the anger. Write a letter if you want to forgive someone; let them know it's all in the past and that you have moved on. If you are too nervous about sending it, just accept that you have forgiven and let go of the past for good. When you can do this, you become a whole person and can love yourself again. You can't love someone who is always blaming others or blaming self, because it's self-defeating.

In the next chapter, I am going to cover goals, because goals help you to love yourself too, but they do need explaining in full, so I am not going to use that in this chapter on self-love. Try to remember what you felt like as a child when you received something that made you feel wonderful inside, or when you saw something that filled you with wonder. Then close your eyes for a moment. You are an incredible human being. Whether you are a believer in a higher power or not, your human body is that of a goddess. It sustains you. It allows you to do so much in your life. You can see, hear, smell, taste, touch, and even sense things in the world around you. Isn't that incredible? What's not to love about something that works in harmony with nature, and that offers you all of these rewards?

All that you need to do to regain self-love is to appreciate who you are. Be thankful when you wake up in the morning and think of all of the things that you are grateful for, as that helps reinforce how wonderful the gift of life is. You were given this gift, and if you can't love it and look after it, then you cannot expect it to know what to do when times get tough. However, if you love it and care for it, it's there to make you a very strong person when life is tough, and to take your hand as you cross the steppingstones of life. You may not know it, but life is what moves you from one steppingstone to the next. Think of it as an invisible friend inside you, giving you strength and love, and when you think of yourself in this way, you can't deny that person that you are the love that you deserve. Self-love has nothing to do with vanity. It has nothing to do with what you own. It has nothing to do with comparisons. It's all about accepting the gift of life and treasuring it.

Chapter Nine: Setting Goals

"If you want to live a happy life, tie it to a goal, not to people or things." – Albert Einstein

What does this have to do with self-esteem? Ask yourself how you feel when you achieve something; even if that achievement is relatively small, you feel good about it because you did it. That's why goals help you to increase your self-esteem. The first time that you do something and finish it, you feel like someone has switched on the light, and it's great to feel capable. This all works toward being a better you, and it also means that you are more accomplished than you were before you did that thing. A child learns all about the world through achievements. The first time a child walks, parents celebrate it. The first time a school kid ties his own laces, that's an achievement that makes the child feel a little less dependent upon adults to do things for him. It continues throughout your life as you accumulate knowledge, but you also need to set yourself small goals if you want your life to go in a forward direction.

When you know what you want in your life, your core goals help you to get there. For example, if you want to travel the world, that first $10 put away in a savings account is a step in the right direction. If you want to become a doctor, aiming at taking the necessary examinations is a stepping stone toward success; all of the things you want to do in life are potentials, and the goals that you make should align with what you want to do. You want to be happier in your life; then, the goal is to meditate daily to help you to become happier in yourself. If you want to live in a nice home, then a goal of decluttering will help you. The goals that take you there don't have to be huge; getting rid of one single bit of clutter is a goal that is taking you in the right direction.

The problem that people with low self-esteem have is that they see the goals in their lives as insurmountable. No goal is insurmountable; it can be broken down into very small tasks that lead you in the direction you want to go. Nothing is beyond the scope of possibility if you start to make small, doable goals. So how do you start with goals if you feel that your self-esteem is low? You decide tonight what you want to do tomorrow. If you can't manage to plan for the whole day, plan for the morning. Then at lunch, make another plan for the afternoon. Goals begin with thinking and then are listed so that you have guidelines of what you are supposed to do. They come in different types too:

- Short term goals – What will you do tonight or tomorrow?

- Medium-term goals – What do you want to achieve this week?

- Long term goals – What dreams do you have for the future?

I would suggest that you start with small goals, and as you gain confidence, start to plan medium-term goals, and then eventually, it will come naturally that long term goals help you to steer your life in the direction you want it to go. It helps your self-esteem and helps you to respect who you are if you set goals and then get to cross them out as you achieve them, but beware; if you get over-ambitious and set impossible goals, you set yourself up for failure, which is why I say that you should start your goal-setting with small things that you can easily manage and then work toward goals that are a little harder.

There are no excuses for not reaching your goals. For example, if you don't do all of the things you have on your list, then the reason is that you set your expectations too high and should start with smaller goals. It's no one's fault. It's just that you have not become accustomed to goalkeeping, so don't beat yourself up if you fail on the first couple of attempts. The idea is always to be realistic in your goals. For example, these could include things that seem relatively mundane, but when you add all of the small achievements together, they all make you feel better about yourself. Here are a few examples that you can use, or you can make goals that are more relevant to your particular case:

- I will clean my shoes tomorrow

- I will leave the kitchen clean after breakfast

- I will set my clothes out tonight for tomorrow

- I will go to bed at ten o'clock tonight

- I will eat more vegetables today

- I will cut out the snacks this morning

- I will smoke less this morning

These may not appear to be much to do, but I don't know the level of your self-esteem, so it's important to start with basic goals before you work your way to more serious goals. The above goals are simply to demonstrate the kind of things that you can use as your goals. Perhaps you neglect yourself, and your goals could include:

- I will wash my hair today

- I will make sure to apply my skin cream

- I will wear make-up today

You make the rules, but when you achieve a goal, you use a big red pen to strike those items off your list that you have achieved. The idea is to try to strike off all of the items on the list that you have made for yourself. If you give priority to these tasks, you will find that you achieve them when you don't allow the interruptions of life get in the way.

As far as work goes, perhaps some goals will help you to achieve more. For example, if you use a system whereby you work without any interruption for a set amount of time in the morning, you achieve more. Hence, turn off telephones or put them onto voicemail. Don't look at your cell phone and certainly do not think of looking at social media during this time. Give yourself a goal of one hour of concentrated work; it's great to stand up and have a break halfway through, and then go back to that concentrated work on the more complex items that you have to do. The reason these goals are great in the morning is that after your meditation, your mind is refreshed and has its highest energy levels, so difficult tasks are easier to perform.

You may want to have a goal about the way that you interact with other people within the work environment. Many people are unhappy at work and don't interact in a friendly way with others. A smile at someone can go a very long way, so make this a goal. Perhaps you see someone struggling with their workload and can help out. Make helpfulness a daily goal, and no matter how small your helpfulness is, it counts. For example, getting your boss a cup of coffee is kind, but so is helping a colleague with a problem. Make a goal of including two acts of kindness within your day and feel good when you achieve that.

You can even stretch this to more acts of kindness at a later date, and this will help your self-esteem levels.

The goals that you set long term should include making your dreams come true. If you want to do something that costs money, then look at savings you can make on things that don't matter that much to you. You will have more money in the long term by deciding to cut down on something today. Perhaps you don't even enjoy your TV much. Limit viewing and save electricity, and free up time to do something more constructive. Perhaps you don't need to pay for all those extra channels you don't even watch. What about your phone contract? Do you need to pay as much as you are? When you have long term goals, you tend to think more in terms of economic adjustments you can make to get to the long-term goals more easily. Goals help your self-esteem, but they also help you to find some sense in your life and reasons for doing what you do.

If you find that you have neglected valuable friendships, you could make a goal to telephone or visit that friend, and at the same time, reinforce the friendship, which is also good for your self-esteem. If you have a free weekend, why not help out at a local dog shelter? This kind of activity may not fit with your long-term goals, but it's great for your self-esteem and helps you to feel that your life is purposeful. There are so many goals that you can set, and you can even split these into different categories such as:

- Relationship goals

- Work goals

- Personal development goals

Relationship goals are important because one phone call can make a world of difference in the way that you feel, and being in touch with positive people will also help your self-esteem. Relationship goals can even include your relationship with yourself because you have to be happy with that before you can work on more serious goals that involve others.

Work goals mean going out of your way to prove your worth, even if only to yourself. Whatever you are capable of within the workplace, make it a priority to do the best that you can during working hours, so that you maximize your opportunities to be relied upon and for promotion. Let everyone know your worth simply by doing the job right, and you don't need anyone's validation. Your goals will tell you how well you are doing, and you can always up the ante when the goals are too easy to achieve.

Personal development goals:

- Looking your best
- Optimizing the way that you present yourself to the world
- Learning something new so that you don't stagnate
- Doing something each day that is pure pleasure for you

There are so many things that people want to include in their lives, but they find that there isn't time to do those things. You have to make small goals that lead you to open up your full potential. For example, why not listen to a language course while commuting to work? What about stopping by the gym on the way home? How about reading the book you have been promising you will read and giving yourself some downtime to do things that make a great difference to your life? Learning is always going to make you feel more valuable because the knowledge that you gain during your life is so useful to you. It can also give you a real sense of achievement.

No matter how small your goals are when you start to use goals for personal development, they are helping you to move toward bigger and better goals, but the biggest boost you get from goal-achieving is that you can actually see yourself improving and get a real buzz out of striking those goals off your list.

You are a wonderful human being but have perhaps inherited goals that do not suit you. These are your choices from now on. Walk with faith in your heart that you can make goals and keep them so that you become an achiever, and with that achievement, become self-assured and self-confident. The purpose of a goal is to give you a direction to your life, and no matter how small those goals may be, a sense of direction gets you there faster.

For the time being, sit down with your notepad and write down the goals for tomorrow morning. Try to achieve them. Don't be too ambitious. If you are not already a goal-oriented woman, it will take time to get there, but little goals and achievements will enthuse you sufficiently to make bigger goals and to experience bigger achievements.

Remember not to weigh yourself down with so many goals that you cannot possibly achieve them. A few for tomorrow morning will lead to a few for tomorrow afternoon. As you make this habit stick, you will find that your goals become your rewards and that your life takes on a new meaning and order, where all things become possible. Do not limit yourself by setting out on a journey without knowing where you are heading.

Conclusion

"The very least you can do in your life is to figure out what you hope for. And the most you can do is live inside that hope. Not admire it from a distance but live right in it, under its roof." - Barbara Kingsolver

Now that you have read through the chapters of this book, that doesn't mean the work is finished. It is only just beginning. The tools that you will need to make all of this work are the following:

• A notebook - to write down your progress, to keep notes and to list goals

• A red marker - to cross off your goals as you achieve them

• A meditation space - to give you the peace of mind you need to move forward

I would also ask that you go back through the chapters and take notes of those areas that affect you or that you feel will help you to develop your self-esteem. It is easy to look backward in life and regret things that have happened. It's far harder to forgive and move on, but when you take the route that is suggested in this book, you will find you are not alone. There are thousands of women out there in the world with whom you can share what you learn. Not only will this help your self-esteem, but it will also give you purpose and a very good reason to continue the habits that are outlined in Chapter Six. However, before you get there, the idea of Chapter Four was to introduce you to yourself, and that's an extremely important part of fixing your self-esteem because the physiological working of the human body may be what is holding you back. The care that you give to your body counts when it comes to feeding the body with all of the fuel it needs to present you to the world as a complete and happy human being.

You have learned the part that the brain plays in self-esteem, and that's an important lesson. Don't hesitate to go back to the chapters to reinforce your values and to ensure that you stick to the suggested habits. You are more in control of things than you give yourself credit for. Although parts of the book relate to anxiety and fears, knowing how your body works helps you to understand the reactions that you live with every day of your life. Those fears could be controllable as could the anxiety, just by knowing what's going on inside you and why you feel that momentary panic in the first place.

I want you to shine. I want you to be able to move on from reading this book to a better understanding of life because, at the end of the day, your life counts from the moment you decide to make it count. Start to plan your journey. Start to realize what your long-term ambitions are and make your life head in the right direction.

The most important aspect of all of this is that you are now living in the moment. What happened to you in the past only remains a part of you for as long as you allow it to. Now is the time to forgive and move on so that the events of the past do not dictate your level of self-esteem today. Think of self-esteem as the way that you look at yourself, and when you start to respect yourself and see good things, then you will find that those around you respect that Goddess that you may have kept hidden until now.

There is a lot of reference material within the book, and it's worthwhile following the links to the suggested YouTube videos as these are an important part of reinforcing what was said within the pages of the book. Learning to care for yourself is part of the journey; if you stop along the way to enjoy a sunset or to eat an ice-cream, then good for you! It is spontaneous acts of joy that make your world a better place and inspire you to carry on positively.

I am happy that you read the book cover to cover and that you have arrived here, at the end of the book, but at the beginning of a new understanding of who you are as a woman, and that you can now go forward with the guidance of the book. Self-esteem and confidence are worked on for the simple reason that life chips away at them, and although some women already know the remedy to fight back, others are not as aware of what helps to mend those chinks in their armor. Now you are, and I hope that you move forward, proud of what you learned and able to live the life that you fully deserve.